D0608457

Phil Chambers is Chief Arbiter of the World Memory Sports Council, and a member of both the Professional Speaking Association and MENSA (the high IQ society). He is the only person to have received the Brain Trust's Special Services to Memory award twice and he has been honoured with the Officer's Cross of the Companionate of the White Swan for services to global mental literacy.

Twice World Mind Mapping Champion and one of the longest established Buzan Master Trainers, Phil frequently delivers Mind Mapping, Memory and Speed Reading programmes alongside Tony Buzan. He has contributed to many of his books, including *Use Your Head*, *Mind Maps for Business*, *The Mind Map Book* and Buzan's official biography.

Phil has also authored or co-authored seven books: *The Student Survival Guide*, *A Mind to Do Business*, *101 Top Tips for Better Mind Maps*, *The Memory Arbiters' Handbook*, *The Memory Yearbook*, *Brilliant Speed Reading* and *How to Remember Equations and Formulae*.

He has a wealth of experience, having delivered training for corporations, schools, universities and charitable organizations, as well as individual coaching on a one-to-one basis. He has worked in many countries including China, Japan, Russia, India, the USA, the Middle East and throughout Europe and been interviewed on BBC TV and Radio.

How to: ACADEMY launched in September 2013. Since then it has organized over 400 talks and seminars on Business, Lifestyle, and Science & Technology, which have been attended by 40,000 people. The aim of the series is to anticipate the needs of the reader by providing clarity, precision and know-how in an increasingly complex world.

PHIL CHAMBERS

HOW TO: TRAIN YOUR MEMORY

bluebird
books for life

First published 2017 by Bluebird
an imprint of Pan Macmillan
20 New Wharf Road, London N1 9RR
Associated companies throughout the world
www.panmacmillan.com

ISBN 978-1-5098-1455-8

Copyright © How To Academy Limited 2017

The right of Phil Chambers to be identified as the
author of this work has been asserted by him in accordance
with the Copyright, Designs and Patents Act 1988.

All rights reserved. No part of this publication may be reproduced,
stored in a retrieval system, or transmitted, in any form, or by any means
(electronic, mechanical, photocopying, recording or otherwise)
without the prior written permission of the publisher.

Pan Macmillan does not have any control over, or any responsibility for,
any author or third-party websites referred to in or on this book.

9 8 7 6 5 4 3 2 1

A CIP catalogue record for this book is available from the British Library.

Printed and bound by CPI Group (UK) Ltd, Croydon, CR0 4YY

This book is sold subject to the condition that it shall not, by way of
trade or otherwise, be lent, hired out, or otherwise circulated without
the publisher's prior consent in any form of binding or cover other than
that in which it is published and without a similar condition including
this condition being imposed on the subsequent purchaser.

Visit **www.panmacmillan.com** to read more about all our books
and to buy them. You will also find features, author interviews and
news of any author events, and you can sign up for e-newsletters
so that you're always first to hear about our new releases.

This book is dedicated to

the memory of my father,

RON CHAMBERS

26/8/1928–23/11/2015

EDINBURGH LIBRARIES	
C0047464585	
Bertrams	03/10/2017
	£6.99
BH	BF385

Contents

Foreword

With a wealth of experience of accelerated learning techniques, Phil Chambers makes the ideal teacher. As well as being a practitioner of neuro-linguistic programming (NLP), he teaches speed reading, and is the World Mind Mapping Champion and a Tony Buzan Master Trainer.

For the past couple of decades Phil has travelled the globe in his capacity as Chief Arbiter for the World Memory Sports Council. He has organized and judged memory competitions at the highest level, which has enabled him to gain an in-depth knowledge and understanding of the most powerful techniques that competitors, such as myself, have used to become World Memory Champions.

In 2008 I co-founded the UK Schools Memory Championships and Phil Chambers was instrumental in organizing the resources for teaching specialized memory techniques to thousands of students and their teachers.

The goal was, and still is, simple: by playing the 'game of memory' students learn to develop and enhance their working memory so that they can study more efficiently and pass exams. In this way they are able to improve their prospects of success both in the classroom and later on in the workplace. Perhaps the most valuable benefits that come from mastering these techniques are that learning becomes 'fun', and the stress that so often accompanies traditional rote-learning methods is removed.

Working memory, the brain's ability to memorize, organize and recall information, is at its centre. Training one's working memory has powerful implications for learning and I believe that our brains keep on growing and maturing as we age. It is now being suggested that a person's working memory is a better predictor of academic success, indeed success in later life, than IQ.

Whether you are a student looking for a shortcut to exam success, a professional hoping to store a vast array of facts and figures or a senior citizen wanting to maintain a healthy, reliable memory, this book crystallizes the most effective memory methods and systems, providing the reader with an array of skills to remember historical facts, names and faces, passwords, speeches without notes and much more.

The real pay-off is that, once learned, these simple memory tools make everyday life so much easier.

How to Train Your Memory is a treasure trove of tips and tricks to help you develop a powerful memory and give you the confidence to tackle any subject, and it is with delight that I recommend this book to you.

Dominic O'Brien
Eight times World Memory Champion

INTRODUCTION

Do you ever lose your car keys, phone or glasses and have to spend ages looking for them? These are small items and it's understandable that they may get overlooked. Your car, on the other hand, weighs over a tonne and is a huge lump of glass and metal. How can you forget where you left something that big? Most of us have done that at one time or another.

Have you walked into a room and wondered what you went in for? Have you had a long conversation with someone you've met before, perhaps even more than once, having absolutely no idea of his or her name? Worse still, have you been introduced to someone and forgotten their name thirty seconds later?

Don't worry. You're not going senile. It's not even old age. Go into an average primary school after home time and see what's been left behind. You'll find pencil cases, bags, coats, PE kit, books, gloves and numerous other items. Kids don't worry about their memories. Everyone has momentary lapses of memory, even World Memory Champions. Ben Pridmore, three times champion, has almost lost count of how many lucky hats he's left on trains.

If you use the techniques in this book, you will be able to remember anything you want to. This can help you in business, in relationships, and in your daily life. You will never forget a client's name, an important birthday or anniversary, or what you need to buy in the supermarket.

Why train your memory?

What is the point of remembering anything when there are devices that store everything we need to know? A Google search will quickly find the answer to almost any question. Our phones store all the numbers we need. A simple paper diary or a more sophisticated PDA (personal digital assistant) or app such as Evernote will store thoughts, appointments and other useful data. We are even alerted to friends' birthdays on Facebook. In the modern world, it seems that memory is redundant, but there are reasons why training your memory can have a huge impact on your life.

1. Start innovating

We live in a world where information is readily available and thus relatively cheap. At the same time creativity and innovation are in great demand and highly valued. Innovation relies on combining concepts and knowledge in novel ways to create new products or ideas. If all your knowledge comes from Internet searches and little is retained, then the data remains discrete and largely unconnected. The synthesis required to innovate is broken. The more information you can hold in your memory, the more you have to work with in order to make informed decisions and come up with new ideas.

2. Build relationships

Business is built on relationships. The word 'company', meaning 'a business entity with an aim of making a profit', derives from the same Latin root as 'companion'. In any business interaction, especially sales, remembering someone's name, together with some personal details, builds trust and rapport: people feel impressed and flattered that you have taken sufficient time and interest in them. Conversely, meeting someone whilst struggling to remember his or her name is embarrassing and awkward. With a few simple techniques, outlined in Chapter Six of this book, names will become easy to memorize and almost effortless to recall.

3. Strengthen your mind and get smarter

The brain is like a muscle: the more you exercise it, the stronger it gets. Professor Mark Rosenzweig from the University of California performed experiments comparing the brains of rats raised in normal cages to those in enriched environments with wheels, tunnels, ladders and other toys to play with. His findings showed that, even in adulthood, greater stimulation leads to an increase in the volume of the cerebral cortex. Rather than filling up your brain like a filing cabinet, training it makes it bigger.

Research by Dr Tracy Alloway from the University of North Florida suggests that training your working memory improves your fluid intelligence,[1] which is your ability to solve problems in novel situations. Memory training literally makes you smarter.

4. Create and recreate

Improving your memory involves use of your imagination and creativity – just like daydreaming. When you recall information you recreate the imagined scenes laid down in your mind whilst memorizing. This recreation is fun! It may sound frivolous and counterproductive to be talking about daydreaming: surely this has no place in business and is a childish weakness? The opposite is actually true. Giving yourself permission to play and be *childlike*, not childish, is vital to memory and creativity. As Frederic Nietzsche put it, 'A person's maturity consists in having found again the seriousness one had as a child, at play.'

What is memory?

There are many different ways to classify memory, and one categorization is that of 'procedural' versus 'declarative'. Procedural memories are physical skills, like riding a bicycle or playing the piano. These non-conscious memories are stored in different regions of the brain and undergo quite different processes to declarative memories. They are typically acquired through repetition and practice.

The mnemonic (memory) techniques in this book deal with declarative memories. These are memories that can be consciously recalled (or 'declared'). They can be sub-categorized into 'semantic' and 'episodic' memories.

Semantic memories are facts, figures and concepts. These are the things you are expected to learn for exams.

Episodic memories are memories of events (or 'episodes'). These are easily and naturally stored. Can you remember the most recent holiday you took, or where you met your partner? You stored these memories in perfect detail without having to learn them.

Most of the techniques that I will teach you involve converting semantic information into episodic memories. The brain treats vividly imagined experiences exactly the same way as real experiences and thus stores them without effort. By substituting words and numbers with people and objects we can easily and quickly remember anything we need.

Memories are initially fragile and need to be reinforced to be sustained. To transfer information from short-term to long-term memory, you need to review it. To be most efficient, you have to review at the correct intervals. If you leave it too late to review, you will have started to forget and will need to do a lot of relearning. If you review too frequently, you may be spending more time than you need. In Chapter Nine we will explore the psychology behind spaced reviews and reveal how it only takes five reviews to make a memory permanent.

This book is the culmination of my quarter-century love affair with the study of memory, as well as more than twenty years of teaching memory-improvement techniques. Memory impacts all aspects of human existence, from who you are, to your relationships with the people you meet and the success you have in school, business and daily life. A trained memory can improve your life, make you smarter and impress your friends. Enjoy the book, playing games with your imagination as you boost your memory!

Record breakers

To see what is possible with a highly trained memory we need to consider some of the world record holders.

On 1 May 2002, as celebrations and parades took place in London, a momentous memory feat was underway in the seclusion of the basement rooms of famous restaurant Simpsons-in-the-Strand.

Eight times World Memory Champion Dominic O'Brien sat silently turning over playing cards one at a time in a neat stack, closely observed by me and a small group of fellow official arbiters. Dominic was not permitted to look back at any of the cards. Once he turned a card, he had to commit it to memory. Periodically he would get up from the desk, sit in an armchair and, eyes closed, mentally review the cards so far.

After the memorization was complete came the moment of truth: the recall. Dominic sat with his back to me. I held each set of cards. Dominic would tell me the card. I turned it over, waited for a second so he could correct a possible slip of the tongue with his answer, and then said, 'correct' or 'wrong'.

In fewer than sixteen hours, Dominic had memorized 2,808 cards – fifty-four inter-shuffled packs – with only eight errors, four of which he guessed correctly at a second attempt. With this powerful memory, it is little wonder that Dominic is banned from casinos worldwide for card-counting whilst playing Blackjack in Las Vegas.

World Memory Championships

Founded in 1991, the annual World Memory Championships test competitors over the course of three gruelling days in ten memory disciplines:

Names and Faces

Binary Digits

Random Numbers

Abstract Images

Speed Numbers

Historic/Future Dates

Random Cards

Random Words

Spoken Numbers

Speed Cards (one deck against the clock)

Despite the challenging nature of the event, Guinness World Records are broken every year and the boundaries of mental achievement are pushed ever further.

In 2015, amongst the most impressive performances was that of the American Alex Mullen, the eventual winner, who memorized 3,029 random numbers in one hour. There was also a great achievement, breaking a very long-standing record, on the order of shuffled decks of playing cards in a set period of time. The new record of 1,612 cards (thirty-one decks) in one hour was set by Shi Binbin from the 2015 host nation, China.

The people who set records do not have photographic memories – a trait that most scientists believe to be a myth. They are ordinary people who have learned exactly the same techniques that you will find in this book. The only difference is that, like physical athletes, they have put in hours of dedicated practice to hone their skills.

1:

LINGUISTIC MEMORY SYSTEMS

Most people think of memory techniques (also known as mnemonics) as phrases or 'tricks' with words. This book will mostly cover more sophisticated methods based on the use of imagination and association. However, in some instances linguistic methods can be useful. Linguistic methods fall into essentially four distinct categories: acronyms, acrostics, rhymes and use of words to represent numbers. We'll look at each in turn. It can take some time to devise an effective linguistic mnemonic but as it doesn't require you to learn any specific new skill, you can start right away. You can be as playful and creative as you like. If you enjoy solving puzzles and crosswords, you will probably enjoy these techniques. Despite being effective, they are not infallible and I will point out some of the potential weaknesses in each technique.

Acronyms

An acronym is formed by taking the initial letters of a phrase to make up a new word. I am sure you're familiar with BBC (British Broadcasting Corporation), NATO (North Atlantic Treaty Organization) or SCUBA (self-contained underwater breathing apparatus). In a world of texting, conversations can consist of lots of acronyms. Phrases like 'oh my god' and 'laugh out loud' become 'OMG' and 'LOL'. Such abbreviations are nothing new. 'TTFN' represented the phrase 'Ta Ta For Now', a catchphrase popularized by comedian Tommy Handley in his 1940s radio show entitled *ITMA*, an acronym itself for *It's That Man Again*.

Every profession or industry has its own acronyms, and none more so than computing and telecommunications. Take 'ADSL', the standard used for much broadband internet access, which stands for 'asymmetric digital subscriber line'. 'JPEG', a common image format, stands for the developers of the standard, the 'Joint Photographic Experts Group'. 'HTML', the code behind websites, is 'HyperText Markup Language'. Many years ago I used to work as a mainframe computer programmer and I remember there being hundreds of 'TLA's and 'FLA's – that's 'three-letter acronyms' and 'four-letter acronyms'!

So how can we use acronyms to help our memories? Acronyms work because they shorten a complex list into a simple word that is easier for our minds to deal with. For example, the North American Great Lakes can be recalled by the simple word 'HOMES' – Huron, Ontario, Michigan, Erie and Superior. Of course, you need to know the names of the lakes first but the acronym helps bring them back to mind.

You may be familiar with the word 'BODMAS', which helps you remember the order in which to solve arithmetic problems. Brackets (parts of a calculation inside brackets always come first) then orders (numbers involving powers or square roots), division, multiplication, addition and finally subtraction.

It is remarkable how powerful acronyms can be in cementing a memory. Thirty years ago, when I was in primary school, a big, fat, jolly community policeman known as PC 'Slim' Cooper would visit the school on his bicycle to teach the kids about playing safely and not talking to strangers. As part of his talk he would explain road safety with the acronym 'SPLINK'. I can still remember it stands for the following points:

Find a **S**afe place to cross away from **P**arked cars,
Look left and right,
If **N**othing is coming, start to cross,
Keep looking and listening.

A few years later, when I was at secondary school and learning French, I was taught the list of verbs that take *être* in the perfect tense by the acronym 'DRAPER'S VAN MMRT'. This stands for:

Descendre
Retourner
Arriver
Partir
Entrer
Rester
Sortir
Venir
Aller
Naître
Monter
Mourir
Rentrer
Tomber

An alternative could be 'MRS VANDERTRAMP'. This is especially good as it is a very unusual name and hence will stick in your mind. If you have a list you need to know, try to arrange the items into an order that will spell out a silly-sounding word.

You can reverse the process of forming acronyms to help with difficult-to-spell words or technical terminology. Rather than using initial letters to remember a list or phrase, you use a phrase to remember the letters of a word. For example, to help a child remember how to spell 'because' you can say, 'Big Elephants Can't Always Use Small Exits'. However, you don't always need a full acronym to give a sufficient prompt to a spelling. To remember that the word 'embarrass' has two letter 'R's and two 'S's you can use the phrase: 'I turn Really Red when my Sister Sings'. Finally, if you struggle to distinguish between 'desert' and 'dessert', you can remember that a desert has Sand (one 'S') and a dessert has Sweet Stuff (two 'S's).

Acrostics

An acrostic is defined as 'a poem or other form of writing in which the first letter, syllable or word of each line, paragraph or other recurring feature in the text spells out a word or a message'. In the case of a memory system, the series of letters spelt out corresponds to the initial letters of the list to be recalled. For example:

My
Very
Easy
Method
Just
Speeds

Up

Naming

Planets

corresponds to:

Mercury

Venus

Earth

Mars

Jupiter

Saturn

Uranus

Neptune

Pluto

I know Pluto is no longer regarded as a planet but the technique still holds true.

There are many variations on acrostics that can be applied to a wide variety of subjects. The technique is effectively used by medical students to memorize anatomy, though many of their examples are too risqué to be repeated here!

One of the benefits of this technique is that it is relatively straightforward to create a meaningful sentence based on a series of letters so it is easier to devise than an acronym. For example, below are the trigonometric ratios followed by two examples of acrostics which represent them:

Sine = Opposite / Hypotenuse

Cosine = Adjacent / Hypotenuse

Tangent = Opposite / Adjacent

Senior Officers Have
Curly Auburn Hair
Till Old Age

Should Old Harry
Catch Any Herrings
Trawling Off America

They can be written in a different order in the form Opposite / Hypotenuse = Sine, etc.

One Ancient Teacher
Of History Swore
At His Charges

Here are some further examples of acrostics:

Geology

The order of geological time periods: Cambrian, Ordovician, Silurian, Devonian, Carboniferous, Permian, Triassic, Jurassic, Cretaceous, Palaeocene, Eocene, Oligocene, Miocene, Pliocene, Pleistocene, Recent.

Cows Often Sit Down Carefully. Perhaps Their Joints Creak? Persistent Early Oiling Might Prevent Painful Rheumatism.

Botany/Zoology

Remembering the classification system of: Kingdom, Phylum, Class, Order, Family, Genus, Species.

Kings Play Chess On Fine Glass Sets.

What could go wrong?

One disadvantage of both acronyms and acrostics is that there is usually no indication of what each letter corresponds to. If the same letter occurs more than once, there is no way of knowing which possibility is correct. This is shown in the following example. This acrostic is used to recall the system of colour-coded stripes used in electronics to indicate degree of resistance. It is possible to confuse brown with black or even blue as all begin with the letter 'B', and green with grey as both begin with 'G'.

Bye
Bye
Rosie
Off
You
Go (to)
Birmingham
Via
Great
Western

represents:

Black
Brown
Red
Orange
Yellow
Green
Blue
Violet
Grey
White

This can be resolved by including one or more of the same words in the acrostic as in the data to be recalled. For example, to remember the colours of the visible spectrum:

>Violets
>In
>Boxes
>Give
>You
>Odours
>Rare

leads to:

>Violet
>Indigo
>Blue
>Green
>Yellow
>Orange
>Red

or in the reverse order:

>Read
>Out
>Your
>Green
>Book
>In
>Verse

Another potential pitfall of acrostics is the possibility of paraphrasing rather than recalling the exact wording. This example is used to remember the lines of the treble music staff EGBDF.

Every
Good
Boy
Deserves
Fudge

It would make just as much sense to misquote 'All Good Boys Deserve Fudge' which would lead to AGBDF.

Try making up acrostics for any list-based information you need in your job, studies or hobbies. I have created the following to help recall Meredith Belbin's nine team roles in management theory.

Teams
Can
Sometimes
Seem
Complete
If
People
Make
Relationships

represents:

Teamworker
Co-ordinator
Specialist
Shaper
Completer/Finisher
Implementer
Plant
Monitor/Evaluator
Resource investigator

Rhymes

Do you find it easy to remember song lyrics or favourite poems? The tune, rhythm, rhyme and intonation give your brain extra associations to help you memorize the words.

Have you come across the following old rhyme?

> Thirty days hath September,
> April, June, and November,
> All the rest have thirty-one,
> Except February alone,
> Which has but twenty-eight days clear,
> And twenty-nine in each leap year.

Another commonly known example is 'In 1492, Columbus sailed the ocean blue.' You sometimes need to take care. In this instance 1482 would also rhyme so there is scope to misremember.

Rhymes can be used for almost any subject, even simple mathematical formulae, e.g. 'If you need a round hole repaired, the formula is πr^2.'

Google 'Richard Digance Sod's Law' for a good example featuring the physical laws of Newton, Einstein, Pythagoras and Archimedes. It does contain some moderately bad language, so be warned. Also see 'Galaxy DNA Song' by Eric Idle and John Du Prez, written for the BBC series *Wonders of Life* with Professor Brian Cox.

You can make up songs, verses or poems as a fun way to memorize complex information. I once taught the main points of the Crime and Disorder Act 1998 to the tune of 'A Policeman's Lot is not a Happy One' from Gilbert and Sullivan's *The Pirates of Penzance*.

Representing numbers

If you need to remember numbers, there are various techniques available that we will discuss in Chapters Three and Five. A linguistic approach is to represent each digit by a word with the corresponding number of letters. For example, the first fifteen digits of Pi (3.14159265358979) can be recalled with the following: *'How I need a drink, alcoholic of course, after the heavy chapters involving quantum mechanics.'*

As you can't get a word with no letters, you can represent zero with a ten-letter word. Here are two more examples:

The square root of two is approximately 1.414
and can be recalled with:
I wish I knew (the root of two).

The base of natural logarithms known as 'e'
is approximately 2.7182818. This can be recalled
using the apt sentence:
To express e remember to memorize a sentence.

It takes quite a bit of ingenuity to create these kinds of linguistic devices. It can be an interesting exercise, but the other number techniques we will cover later are more practical.

A major problem with linguistic mnemonics as a whole is that they do not allow you to build on the basic information or add additional facts. Consider the acrostic above used to remember the order of the planets of the solar system. There is no way to add details of approximate sizes, whether they have rings or moons, atmospheric conditions, colours and probes that have visited each. In the next chapter we will introduce the concept of linking that can, to some extent, overcome this limitation.

Summary

- An acronym is a word made up of the initial letters of a phrase or list to be memorized.

- An acrostic is a form of writing in which the first letter of each line corresponds to the initial letters of the list to be memorized.

- Rhymes are verses or songs linking information often, though not exclusively, in couplets.

- You can remember long numbers by representing each digit by a word with a corresponding number of letters.

- Advantages of linguistic memory systems:
  - There is no need to learn any specific new skill so you can start right away.
  - It is relatively straightforward to create a meaningful sentence based on a series of letters.

- Disadvantages of linguistic memory systems:
  - Alternative rhymes can lead to incorrect recall.
  - There is a possibility of paraphrasing rather than recalling the exact wording, leading to errors.
  - It is difficult to link related additional information.

2:

ENHANCED MEMORY SYSTEMS

In this chapter we will look at the basic principles of imagination and association that underpin most of the strategies in the remainder of this book. Along the way we will touch on some of the psychological research into memory, and, finally, I will explain how to practically apply a simple technique to remember a list.

Attention, please!

In the introduction to this book I talked about losing your keys, your phone or your glasses and forgetting where you parked the car. There is a very simple explanation of why this happens and an equally simple remedy.

You are absent-minded!

I'm not casting aspersions on your mental abilities. What I mean is that your mind is elsewhere. When you come home in the evening you are likely to be thinking about what you'll be having for dinner; maybe you are going out that night or you are thinking about your partner or kids. You are almost certainly not thinking about where you put your keys down. At that moment it is unimportant and you pay no attention to it. A couple of hours later, the location of your keys takes on great importance as you need to leave the house. You have no recollection of where they are because the memory was never stored in the first place.

Exactly the same thing happens when you park your car. Every journey has a purpose. You are driving to a location to attend a meeting, go shopping, watch a film at the cinema, whatever. Your thoughts will inevitably be on the purpose of your excursion. You will be anticipating the film, or thinking about the meeting, who'll be there and what will be discussed. Your focus is on the future.

The solution is to bring your mind back to the present for a few seconds. As you walk away from the car, pause and look back at it. Notice the surroundings. What landmarks can you see? Is it near a specific building or a certain tree? What shapes do you notice? Because you are looking back, this will be the same viewpoint you will get when you return. As the brain has registered details of the scene it will recognize them again when you get back and immediately locate your car.

If you park outside, this will work. On the other hand, if you find yourself in a uniformly bland location such as a multi-storey car park where every level looks the same with grey concrete walls and pillars, you will need to remember a level number and maybe an exit designation. Something like 'blue, level four'. In this case, you can use a simple number technique. We will cover this is in the next chapter.

Follow the same process with your keys, phone or glasses. Look at where you put them down and actively notice the location. Is this in the hallway, on the kitchen worktop or on the coffee table in the lounge?

We similarly sabotage our memories when we meet people. When someone introduces him/herself, if you are focusing on what you are going to say next, you are not registering the name. Little wonder you forget it. Many of our so-called failures of memory are actually failures of perception.

Types of memory

When we perceive or experience something the memory of this is what psychologists call 'episodic memory'. It is a brief episode of your life. I am sure you can recall what you did earlier today or where you last went on holiday without much conscious effort.

As long as you notice what is happening, the brain will store it. Memories of this type are strongest when your perception is heightened by shocking or emotionally charged situations. Can you remember your first passionate kiss, what you were doing when you heard the news of Princess Diana's death or the 9/11 attack on the World Trade Center in New York? We only forget mundane, uneventful times. Your memory keeps the edited highlights.

The other main classification of memory is called 'semantic memory'. This is the ability to recall data, facts, figures, appointments and definitions. It is all the stuff you were taught in school and the kind of things you are expected to remember in business. If you've ever watched the BBC TV show *Dragons' Den*, you'll know that any would-be entrepreneur business partner gets short shrift if they can't recall their balance sheet. Without the right techniques, laying down semantic memories is very hard work.

The key to memorizing semantic information is to convert it into an episodic format that is easier to deal with. If you encode what you need to memorize into a vividly imagined experience, the brain treats it in exactly the same way as a real one. There are a wide variety of encoding systems suited to particular types of data and situations that we will explore in future chapters.

Ideasthesia

There are some people for whom the conversion of concepts to experiences happens naturally. This is a condition called 'ideasthesia' where a concept automatically triggers a sensory response. One common manifestation of this is where numbers or letters of the alphabet are associated with vivid experiences of colour. Nobel prizewinning physicist Richard Feynman described what he experiences: 'When I see equations, I see the letters in colors – I don't know why. As I'm talking, I see vague pictures of Bessel functions from Jahnke and Emde's book, with light-tan j's, slightly violet-bluish n's, and dark brown x's flying around. And I wonder what the hell it must look like to the students.'[2] There are many similar examples found in language. For instance, if you say you are in a 'blue' mood, then you have not literally changed colour. Sharp words are not literally like razorblades.

Studies have shown that almost everyone displays ideasthesia to a certain extent. Look at the shapes below. One of them is called 'Kiki' and the other 'Bouba'. Which shape goes with which name?

Did you name the curvy shape as 'Bouba' and the jagged one as 'Kiki'?

This effect was first observed by Wolfgang Köhler in 1929.[3] In 2001, V. S. Ramachandran and Edward Hubbard repeated Köhler's experiment using American university undergraduates and Tamil speakers in India. In both groups, 95–98 per cent of people assigned the name 'Bouba' to the more curved shape and 'Kiki' to the jagged one.[4] Not only is this remarkably consistent across languages and cultures but other concepts such as masculine versus feminine have been shown to be associated with the two shapes.[5,6]

Synaesthesia

A related condition called 'synaesthesia' combines two or more senses. Stimulus of one sense leads to the involuntary concurrent experience in another sense.

It is interesting that many successful composers, musicians and artists have the condition. Stevie Wonder, Kanye West and Pharrell Williams all see sounds and music as colours. Artist David Hockney has similar experiences:

> Hockney sees synesthetic colors to musical stimuli. In general, this does not show up in his painting or photography artwork too much. However, it is a common underlying principle in his construction of stage sets for various ballets and operas, where he bases the background colors and lighting upon his own seen colors while listening to the music of the theater piece he is working on.[7]

An example of a remarkable individual with very strong

synaesthesia and a memory capacity which 'had no distinct limits' is Solomon Shereshevsky, known as S. in studies by Russian psychologist Alexander Luria.[8]

S. was a failed musician who worked as a newspaper reporter in Moscow in the mid-1920s. Each morning the editor would assign various stories to each of the staff. It was noted that S. never took notes during these meetings. When challenged, to the amazement of the editor, he was able to recite everything that had been said in perfect detail. S. didn't see it as remarkable as he thought everybody's memory worked like this. He was sent to meet Luria where he undertook memory tests involving words, numbers and letters. He completed these perfectly, and so began a thirty-year study.

To S. every sound led to an experience of colours, taste and touch sensations. He described this as follows:

> I recognise a word not only by the images it evokes but by a whole complex of feelings that image arouses. It's hard to express . . . it's not a matter of vision or hearing but some overall sense I get. Usually I experience a word's taste and weight, and I don't have to make an effort to remember it – the word seems to recall itself. But it's difficult to describe. What I sense is something oily slipping through my hand . . . or I'm aware of the slight tickling in my left hand caused by a mass of tiny, lightweight points. When that happens I seem to remember, without having to make the attempt . . .
> (Record of 22 May 1939)

Shereshevsky's synaesthesia allowed him to make additional associations between the words he was asked to memorize. Association is one of the most important factors in memory. To memorize something effectively, associate components together or, even more powerfully, associate new information with something you already know.

Using SEAHORSE principles

The acronym SEAHORSE[9] helps you to remember eight memory principles to strengthen your imagined experiences. Why SEAHORSE? The Latin word for seahorse is 'hippocampus'. This is the name of a structure in the brain known to play a role in the consolidation of information from short-term to long-term memory and in spatial navigation.

Research by Dr Eleanor Maguire and her team at University College London[10] studied the brains of London taxi drivers. In order to obtain a licence to drive a London black cab, drivers must learn 'The Knowledge'. This involves knowing every street, and routes between any two points, within a six-mile radius of Charing Cross. It usually takes around three years of hard training to learn, even using some mnemonic techniques.

Maguire conducted magnetic resonance imaging scans on the brains of sixteen cab drivers. The results showed an increase in size of the posterior of the hippocampus in the cabbies compared with a control group. The size difference was even more pronounced in older drivers who had been working in London for forty years. This shows that, with training, the brain can actually grow and change shape, even in adulthood.

The principles of SEAHORSE are as follows:

Senses

How many senses do you have? Most people would say five: vision, hearing, taste, smell and touch. However, there are more subtle senses. Orientation and balance are determined by the semi-circular canals in your inner ear. The skin gives not just tactile responses such as whether an object is textured or smooth, but also information on temperature. Kinaesthesia is a sense from receptors located in muscles, tendons and joints, stimulated by bodily movements.

When imagining scenes, make vivid use of all your multiple senses. The more real something feels, the stronger it will be remembered. Make images brighter, sounds richer, smells and tastes more intense. Experience touch, temperature, position, movement and balance.

Although repulsive and shocking sensual experiences will be remembered, it is better to use positive and pleasurable sensations. If you imagine new experiences, why would you choose to make them negative ones?

Exaggeration

The brain, and hence your memory, tends to disregard and tune out monotonous stimuli. The banal and everyday are forgotten.

Wolfgang Köhler, who we mentioned in connection with ideasthesia, had a female postdoctoral assistant at the University of Berlin called Hedwig von Restorff. In a paper published in 1933, von Restorff described a phenomenon known as the isolation effect, now known more commonly as the Von Restorff Effect.[11] This states that if an item in a list differs from the surrounding data it will be remembered more strongly.

Read the following list of words:

tree
road
shoe
bus
watch
Mohammed Ali
coat
flower
orange
dog

It is easier to remember 'Mohammed Ali' because he is different from the objects in the list.

The Von Restorff Effect is the reason why highlighting keywords in notes helps you to remember them. Anything that makes something stand out will create a Von Restorff Effect.

Shereshevsky reported a similar phenomenon when memorizing. Luria noted that on one occasion S. missed out the word 'pencil' from a list of words and on another test forgot 'egg'. S. explained why:

> I put the image of the pencil near a fence . . . the one down the street, you know. But what happened was that the image fused with that of the fence and I walked right on past without noticing it. The same thing happened with the word egg. I had put it up against a white wall and it blended in with the background. How could I possibly spot a white egg against a white wall? (Record of December 1932)

S. later explained how he learned to rectify the problem using exaggeration:

> I know I have to be on guard if I'm not to overlook some-thing. What I do now is to make my images larger. Take the word egg I told you about before. It was so easy to lose sight of it; now I make it a larger image, and when I lean it up against a building, I see to it that the place is lit up by having a street lamp nearby . . . I don't put things in dark passageways any more . . . Much better if there's some light around, it's easier to spot then. (Record of June 1935)

The technique of placing things in locations that S. is alluding to will be covered in Chapter Four.

By exaggerating proportion, size or some other quality of an object you introduce novelty and therefore make it more memorable.

Action

If you went to the cinema, you would get involved in the action of the film. However, if you were shown a series of still images, you would be far less engaged. When making up imagined scenes and stories, include motion and involve yourself in the action, experiencing things from your point of view. It is your imagination so you don't have to limit yourself. In your mental movie you are the director and the star. You have an unlimited special effects budget and can be as wild as you like.

Humour

Do you forget jokes? The problem with a joke is that it is a series of statements in a narrative followed by a punchline.

The setup has to be put in place in the correct order for the joke to be funny and make any sense. The kind of humour that aids memory is silly, off-the-wall and surreal – the sort of thing performed and written by Monty Python, Spike Milligan, Kenny Everett, Eddie Izzard, Vic Reeves and Bob Mortimer or Noel Fielding and Julian Barratt (writers of *The Mighty Boosh*). You don't have to be a comic genius – anything that makes you smile, chuckle or even groan will lighten even the dullest material and make it memorable. Research by Schmidt found evidence that funny sentences are more memorable than neutral ones.[12] This is something exploited to great effect in the advertising industry.

Order

Ordered items are easier to recall than those that are jumbled up. The brain likes patterns and logic. If the data has no natural sequence or order, you can create one with a story. This will add flow and meaning. Try to think of a reason for each item following the previous one and interacting. Take care to link each item in turn rather than allowing yourself to return to objects already covered. This strict ordering prevents you from missing out objects and jumping ahead.

Repetition

Repetition is brute force. I am sure you must have experienced going over something again and again until it eventually sticks in your mind. Used in isolation, repetition can be boring drudgery. When used in combination with the other seven principles, it is pleasurable to revisit your imagined stories and scenes.

Have you heard the saying 'practice makes perfect'? This is inaccurate. If you practise the wrong thing, you can be very far from perfection. A more accurate saying would be 'practice makes permanent'.

Repetition has an impact on the physiological nature of your brain. Whenever you have a thought or perform an action, a series of brain cells link up to transmit an electrical signal between them. At each stage making up the circuit there is a gap from one brain cell to the next called a synapse. This gap is bridged by the release of chemicals called neurotransmitters. When you repeat an action the same network is re-activated. The more times you repeat something, the easier it is for the signal to flow as the synapses involved are strengthened. This is known as long-term potentiation. You metaphorically rewire your brain whenever you learn or memorize anything.

Symbols

It is often the case that we have to memorize abstract concepts. These do not immediately lend themselves to sensual, actively imagined scenes. We can overcome this by the use of symbolism: using an object to represent a concept. Symbolism stands in for ideasthesia in the memorizing process. Symbols can be based on the sound of a word or its meaning. For example, you could represent time by imagining a pocket watch, an electrical current with a currant bun, or pressure with a bicycle pump.

Enjoy

Stress and boredom interfere with your memory. You need to adopt a playful attitude. Treat memorizing like a game. If you are enjoying memorizing, you will also enjoy recalling and the process will be much easier. Give yourself permission to free your imagination and be childlike (not childish). The Ancient Greek philosopher Heraclitus of Ephesus said that 'Man is most nearly himself when he achieves the seriousness of a child at play.'

Using the Link System

This is the simplest memory system. All you have to do is use the SEAHORSE principles to make up an imaginative story linking together each item from a list in sequence. You are building a chain of associations. For example, to memorize the following random list:

> spike
> gherkin
> shampoo
> vixen
> tie
> axe
> queen
> hood
> rose
> fire

you could create the following story:

> You are hammering a spike into a gherkin. As it penetrates the vinegar-scented flesh you see shampoo ooze out. Scooping up some of the sticky liquid, you use it to wash a female fox (a vixen). Oddly, the fox is wearing a

tie around its neck like a leash. You set it free by cutting the tie with an axe. The axe is snatched away from you by the queen. She is a wearing a cloak with a hood as a disguise. As she pulls it over her head hundreds of rose petals fall out. Fluttering to the ground, they immediately catch fire on impact.

This is similar to one of the disciplines in Memory Championships where Simon Reinhard from Germany memorized 300 random words in fifteen minutes.

Make up your own story for the following twenty words:

jug
tadpole
treacle
apple
harp
whale
cannon
robot
lolly
airship
alarm
circus
grain
golfer
head
moss
bag
razor
swan
hat

Before recalling, review your story in your mind (principle of repetition). Now cover up the list and try to write them down from memory.

How did you do?

If you forgot any words, consider why this might have been the case. Were your associations too mundane? Did your story meander too much between objects?

A major disadvantage to this system is that if you miss out one of the associations, you break the chain and it is hard to pick up your thread again. In the next chapter I will introduce you to 'Pegging Systems' that overcome this problem.

Summary

- To remember where you left objects, make sure your attention is 'in the moment' when you put them down.

- There are two types of memory:
  – Episodic (concerned with experiences)
  – Semantic (concerned with data)

- To memorize data we convert it into vividly imagined experiences.

- Ideasthesia is the representation of concepts by sensual experiences.

- Synaesthesia is the concurrent experience of multiple senses from a single stimulus.

- Memory systems are based on a combination of imagination and association.

- You can create strong imagined experiences by employing the following eight principles that spell out the acronym SEAHORSE:
  Senses
  Exaggeration
  Action
  Humour
  Order
  Repetition
  Symbols
  Enjoy

- The Link System involves creating a story to form a chain of associations between items in a list, using all the SEAHORSE principles to build vividly imagined scenes.

- The advantage of the Link System is that it is simple and effective.

- The disadvantage of the Link System is that if you miss an item, the chain is broken and it is difficult to continue the story.

3:

LINKING AND PEGGING SKILLS

In this chapter we will look more closely at how to apply the Link System in different situations, including learning languages and English vocabulary. We will then explore the Peg System. You can use this technique to overcome the problem of breaking a chain of associations and finding it hard to pick up your thread again, as identified in Chapter Two. Finally, we will talk about two simple number systems.

Learning foreign languages

I mentioned learning French in Chapter One. I remember my teacher, a Frenchman, who was passionate about his language and hated to hear it mangled by his students, often saying, 'That's not French – it's Chinese.' He had a reputation for his strictness and somewhat fiery temper. In actual fact he wasn't so bad once you got to know him. Every week he would issue a list of vocabulary to learn that would be tested the following week. He always said that the 'village idiot' could learn vocabulary and anyone who didn't was regarded as a slacker. If you failed to get above 80 per cent in the test, you had to come in to school early and sit the test again in his office until you reached the required standard. I really struggled and paid many early morning visits over the course of two years. It did pay off in the end as I got grade 'A' in GCSE French. I now know he was right that anyone can learn vocabulary. I wish I had known how to employ mnemonics at the time.

You can learn vocabulary using a variation of the Link System that we covered in the previous chapter. Instead of forming a chain of associations we just form a single link: symbolize the sound of the word with an object and then link this to an object that represents the meaning. We then continue to use the SEAHORSE principles to form strong links. This technique is known as the 'Linkword. Language System', and was pioneered by Dr Michael M. Gruneberg. It allows you to acquire a large vocabulary very quickly. It doesn't give you conversational fluency but it would have saved me many early mornings at school!

I have included some examples below. In each case the approximate pronunciation is in brackets. It is important to listen to words when memorizing to get the pronunciation correct. There are various websites that play recordings of native speakers saying many words.

Note that these are my immediate associations. You will have your own unique set of associations based on your life experience so they will inevitably be different. When memorizing it is always best to stick with your own ideas and usually first impressions are strongest. For each example, spend a few seconds visualizing the scene.

French

The French for bicycle is *vélo* (vay low)
A bike shop has a sale. Their prices are 'way low'.

The French for milk is *lait* (lay)

Imagine what it would feel like to lay in a bath of milk like Cleopatra.

The French for coat is *manteau* (manto)
Imagine a man with a tiny coat on his toe.

The French for window is *fenêtre* (fen et ra)
Fern-patterned green net curtains at the window.

The French for car is *voiture* (vwat yur)
An angry motorist in a sports car shouts, 'Vhat y'er looking at?'

The French for camel is *chameau* (sham owe)
You have to wash camels with a chamois leather to pay off a debt you owe.

The French for clock is *horloge* (or lorj)
A clock with oars instead of hands. It's large.
(Logically 'horology' is the study and art of clock making.)

The French for candle is *bougie* (boo jee)
A budgie is pecking at a candle. Perhaps he gets his feathers singed.

The French for key is *clé* (clay)
A key made of clay. It is too soft and squidgy to open a lock.

The French for mouth is *bouche* (boosh)
Green leaves of a bush sprouting from someone's mouth.
(Or Noel Fielding, star of the BBC3 TV show
The Mighty Boosh, with a huge mouth.)

German

The German for tortoise is *Schildkröte* (shild krerta)
A tortoise is a shelled critter.

The German for spoon is *Löffel* (lurful)
A spoon full of 'Lurpak' butter. It is lur full.

The German for shark is *Hai* (hi)
Imagine giving a shark a friendly greeting, 'Hi!'

The German for potato is *Kartoffel* (car toffel)
You throw a potato at a cart of offal.

The German for envelope is *Umschlag* (umm shlarg)
You're asked what size envelope you need. You say, 'Um, large'.

The German for egg is *Ei* (eye)
An egg shaped like an eyeball winks at you.

The German for jacket is *Hülle* (hou lur)
A man in a jacket playing with a hula-hoop.

The German for letter is *Brief* (breef)
A letter written on a pair of white briefs.

Italian

The Italian for almond is *mandorla* (mandorla)
Imagine Nelson Mandela eating almonds.

The Italian for blueberry is *mirtilli* (meer til lee)
Moaning Myrtle (from the Harry Potter books) and Christopher Lee picking blueberries.

The Italian for chicken is *pollo* (porlo)
A chicken in an Apollo astronaut's spacesuit.

The Italian for cow is *mucca* (moo ca)
A cow mooing whist driving a car.

The Italian for sheep is *pecora* (pecora)
A sheep with a beak like a woodpecker.

The Italian for garlic is *aglio* (al yo)
Alan Sugar playing with a yo-yo which is a garlic bulb on a string.

The Italian for wall is *muro* (mooro)
A mural on a wall.

The Italian for mouse is *topo* (top oh)
A mouse wearing a top hat.

The Italian for goose is *oca* (or ca)
A goose fighting an orca (killer whale).

The Italian for money is *soldi* (soldi)
A salesman has sold 'de' merchandise and is paid his money.

Spanish

The Spanish for dog is *perro* (perro)
A dog dressed up like a sad clown, a Pierrot.

The Spanish for bull is *toro* (torrow)
The 'Toro Rosso' F1 racing team is Red Bull's second team.

The Spanish for mushroom is *seta* (seta)
A Red Setter dog eating mushrooms.

The Spanish for market is *mercado* (merkado)
The comic opera The Mikado *is performed in the marketplace.*

The Spanish for beach is *playa* (playa)
Play a musical instrument on the beach. Try not to get it covered in sand.

The Spanish for bandage is *venda* (venda)
You buy a bandage from a vending machine.

The Spanish for lunch is *comida* (komeeda)
Imagine being served lunch by your favourite comedian.

The Spanish for monkey is *mono* (mono)
A monkey riding a monocycle.

The Spanish for mother is *madre* (madray)
A mother in a mad rage with you.

The Spanish for curtain is *cortina* (korteena)
Imagine an old Ford Cortina draped with a curtain.

Notice that I have not always used the exact pronunciation in every association. It is supposed to act as a trigger to recall the word. In most cases a vivid visual representation is best although I have occasionally used a logical or linguistic approach.

Try to come up with imaginative links yourself for the following six Swedish words:

The Swedish for ant is *myra* (meera)

The Swedish for bell is *klocka* (kloka)

The Swedish for cuckoo is *gök* (yerk)

The Swedish for duck is *anka* (anka)

The Swedish for eye is *öga* (erga)

The Swedish for rabbit is *kanin* (kaneen)

Mastering gender nouns

Many languages assign gender to nouns. In French, nouns are masculine or feminine and in German you have a third category of neuter. Knowing the gender is very important as it affects several aspects of grammar. In French you have '*le*', '*un*' and '*du*' which are masculine for 'the', 'a' and 'some' and the feminine forms '*la*', '*une*' and '*de la*'. Pronouns, adjectives and verbs take different forms according to the gender of the associated noun. It is evidently very important to learn genders, something that is often a struggle for English speakers.

There are three simple methods you can use.

1. Modify your scene

To denote feminine words modify your imagined scene to include stereotypical feminine associations. Colour things pink, add perfumes and, depending on the scene, add women's clothes or female characters. For example, the French for tablecloth is '*la nappe*'. Imagine a little girl taking a nap with a pink gingham tablecloth as a blanket. Conversely, for male words use stereotypical male associations. Colour things blue and use male clothes and characters. The French for wine is '*le vin*'. A muscular French body builder rips the door of a van from its hinges. Hundreds of bottles of red wine topple out, smashing on the ground, showering you with their sweet smelling, fruity contents.

If you find your scenes populated with men and women are leading to confusion, there is another solution suggested by eight times World Memory Champion Dominic O'Brien.

2. Change location

We will explain the use of location as a general memory technique in Chapter Four. In the context of language learning, Dominic chooses a town or village that he knows well. He then defines an area for male words and another area for female words. So gender is determined by the part of town where the scene is taking place. Maybe all male words are to the west of the high street and all female words to the east. If you are learning German with masculine, feminine and neuter words, then just select three 'zones'.

For example, the French for bread is 'le pain', pronounced 'pan'. So if you have a sandwich shop in the male part of town, you can imagine someone trying to stuff sliced loaves into a big pan on the counter of the shop. 'Le sandwich' is also male. On the female side of town there may be a bakery where you can place French loaves or tarts – 'la baguette', 'la tarte'.

Apart from keeping your nouns contained in set locations, like sheep in a pen, there is an additional benefit to the use of locations. Your memory is triggered each time you are physically in one of those locations so you have a regular episodic review. Imagining nouns of the same gender interacting with each other reinforces your memory of both the meanings and whether they're male or female.

3. Follow signposts of the language

The designation of a gender to a noun is not completely arbitrary. There are some simple rules that can help you deduce the gender of a word and save you the trouble of having to learn each individually. These are only rules of thumb and there are always exceptions, but they work about 80 per cent of the time.

In French, if a noun has the suffix '-ion', it is most likely to be feminine. The majority of words that end in '-e' are also feminine, with the exception of the suffixes '-age', '-ege', '-é' or '-isme' (these often indicate masculine words). All other suffixes are mostly masculine. Similar rules apply in other 'romance' languages.

In Germanic languages, compound words have the same gender as the last word in the compound. Once you know that a 'house' is neuter, you know automatically that all words ending in '-haus' are also neuter. The same rule applies for '-hus' in Danish, for example.

Technical terminology and English vocabulary

A large vocabulary is a great asset in business, education and everyday life.

The same technique of making a link between a word and its meaning can be used to memorize technical or unusual English words. You will need to be especially creative with your symbolism as technical words are often abstract in nature. Here are some examples:

Bathic – adj. – pertaining to depths, especially of

sea. Imagine floating in a very deep bath.
(A bathysphere is a deep-sea submersible and
bathymetry is the process of measuring depths
of sea.)

Pogonophobia – n. – a morbid or irrational fear
of beards. Imagine a bearded man on a pogo-stick.
(Related words: pogonotomy – cutting of a beard,
shaving; pogonotrophy – growing of a beard.)

Ranine – adj. – pertaining to or being similar to
frogs. Imagine you opened your door and a frog
ran in.

Cation – n. – a positively charged atom or molecule.
Imagine a cat with a plus sign painted on its fur.

Many English words, especially scientific or medical
terms, originate from Latin and Greek. Once you know a
few of these they can be broken down and recombined to
deduce the meaning of unfamiliar words.

Take my name, Philip, for example. This is made up of
two Greek words: *philos* ('beloved, loving') and *hippos*
('horse'), so Philip literally means 'fond of horses'. If you
know that anthropology is the study of humans, past and
present, then you can deduce that a 'phil-anthrop-ist' is
someone who loves humanity and promotes or supports
endeavours for the good of mankind. Other words deriving
from the components of my name include:

Francophile – someone who admires France and
the French

Sinophile – someone who admires China and the
Chinese

Philosopher – lover of wisdom. Someone engaged in the academic pursuit of the fundamental nature of knowledge, reality and existence

Hippocampus – 'Seahorse' and especially the sea-horse-shaped structure in the brain that plays a role in laying down new memories, discussed in the previous chapter

Hippopotamus – river horse

Hippophobia – an irrational fear of horses

Vocabulary expands synergistically, meaning that components of words can combine to form many more definitions than the words in isolation. According to Tony Buzan, synergy is a natural function of the human brain.[13]

Pegging

As mentioned in the previous chapter, the problem with the Link System is that there is the possibility of breaking the chain of associations. So far we have looked at single associations between words and their meanings. We can apply the notion of single associations to lists.

Imagine a cloakroom with a series of pegs fixed to the wall. You hang your coat on one of them and leave. When you return the peg hasn't moved and hopefully neither has your coat. A memory 'Peg System' is the use of immovable concepts onto which you hang new information. Memory pegs are things that you know well in a set order. To memorize a list you associate the first item to the first peg, the second item to the second peg and so on. If you forget an item, you have an empty peg. You know you've missed something out but can very easily move on to the next peg. You can also come back to try and fill in any gaps later and knowing what was on either side can often be enough of a prompt to recall anything that was potentially forgotten.

The series of pegs below is associated with the parts of the body. Starting from the ground working up, a body has:

1. Feet
2. Knees
3. Waist / hips
4. Stomach
5. Hands
6. Chest
7. Shoulders
8. Neck
9. Face
10. Hair / top of head

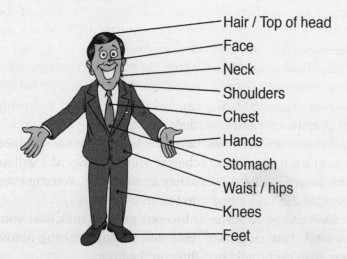

- Hair / Top of head
- Face
- Neck
- Shoulders
- Chest
- Hands
- Stomach
- Waist / hips
- Knees
- Feet

This is enough for a list of ten items but you could extend it to twenty by including: ankles, thighs, buttocks, biceps, forearms, chin, mouth, nose, eyes and ears.

I can demonstrate with a shopping list of ten items:

1. Eggs
2. French loaf
3. Bananas
4. Milk
5. Ham
6. Grapes
7. Mushrooms
8. Cherries
9. Tomatoes
10. Cheese

Associate eggs with feet. Imagine standing on eggs, the smooth shell pressing against your soles. As your full weight bears down on them they crack. You feel the pricking of the broken shell and the contents oozing through your toes. Smell the slightly rotten odour of the eggs.

Associate French bread with knees. Imagine gripping a French loaf between your knees. You have to walk peculiarly to avoid dropping it. You can feel the warmth of its freshly baked crust and smell the delicious aroma.

Bananas and hips. You have bunches of bananas strapped to your hips, perhaps attached to your belt. See the yellow skins flecked with brown as they are very ripe. You can even peel one and take a bite into the creamy flesh.

Milk and your stomach. Imagine pouring milk over your stomach. Tiny rivulets of cold white liquid flowing across your skin, eventually puddling on the floor.

Link ham and hands. Picture yourself juggling whole hams on the bone like clubs.

Grapes and chest. Imagine draping a bunch of grapes over your chest. Feel the woody stalks and the stickiness as some have started to go past their best. Smell the sweet fruity fragrance.

Mushrooms and shoulders. You have mushroom epaulets on your jacket.

Cherries and neck. You're wearing a necklace with bright red cherries instead of beads.

Tomatoes and face. A big red tomato nose like a clown.

Cheese and head. Imagine balancing a whole round cheese on your head. It is especially ripe and stinky.

Simply picture each part of your body and recall which item was placed there. You can easily move forwards and backwards through the list – something that is more difficult to do with the Link System due to its story-like structure.

Number pegging

One issue with body pegging is that it doesn't allow 'random access'. What I mean by this is that, if you want to find the sixth item of the list, you have to count up from one or down from ten. You can't go directly to six. This is not always necessary. However, if you want to be able to do this it is easily accomplished by memorizing a numbered list.

Numbers are abstract concepts so need to be symbolized by objects that can then be linked to in imaginative ways as per the SEAHORSE principles. There are two main systems used to accomplish this.

1. Number Rhyme System

Did you ever learn the following nursery rhyme?

> One, two,
> Buckle my shoe;
> Three, four,
> Open the door;
> Five, six,
> Pick up sticks;
> Seven, eight,
> Lay them straight;
> Nine, ten,
> A big, fat hen.

It is intended to help teach children to count by giving them something to visualize for pairs of digits.

The Number Rhyme System just extends the concept by creating a rhyme for each digit, e.g.:

> zero – hero
>
> one – bun (or sun)
>
> two – shoe
>
> three – tree
>
> four – door
>
> five – hive
>
> six – sticks
>
> seven – heaven
>
> eight – gate
>
> nine – wine (or vine)

2) Number Shape System

This makes an association based on the shape of the number.

> zero – football (or hoop)
> one – candle (or an artist's paintbrush or pencil)
> two – swan
> three – a heart on its side (or an open pair of
>   handcuffs)
> four – sailing dinghy
> five – hook
> six – elephant's trunk curled round to eat (or a
>   snake)
> seven – axe (or a boomerang)
> eight – a snowman (or an hourglass)
> nine (with a straight vertical) – tennis racket

Do you have a to-do list? What happens if you're away from your desk and someone asks you to do something? Do you always remember to add it to your list when you get back?

If you have a great idea which you can't write down because you're driving or in the shower, how can you capture the thought?

Peg Systems are ideal for medium-term memory that you only need to keep for a few hours or a day. The pegs can be reused for new data on an ongoing basis.

Let's say you use the Number Rhyme System to remember the following to-do list:

1. Post a letter
Imagine posting a letter in a bun rather than an envelope.

2. Call a client or a friend
Imagine using your shoe as a phone.

3. Withdraw money from the cash point
Imagine a tree with banknotes as leaves.

4. Write a sales report or letter
Imagine the report nailed to a door.

You pass your boss in the corridor, who says he's been meaning to ask you to email him some figures. You go through the list in your head. Five is a spare space so you imagine a swarm of bees (hive) delivering the figures to your boss.

You are listening to the radio whist driving and hear a review of a play that you'd like to book tickets for when you get home. Once again, run through your list until you find an empty space and make an association between the play and the pegging item.

At some point during the day you mentally run through your pegs making sure you've remembered to do the various tasks.

The following day you need a new list, so you leave the Number Rhyme System to one side and use Number Shapes. As we will see in Chapter Nine, memories decay very quickly if not reviewed. Having left your Rhyme pegs alone for a day, any associations will have started to fade. This means you can overwrite them with new associations on the third day. You can have a rolling to-do list alternating between rhymes and shapes with up to ten items per day.

Other applications of numbers

Having created a series of associations for the digits zero to nine, we can use them in a normal Link System fashion to remember short numbers.

You can't use rhymes or shapes for long numbers like telephone numbers, bank account details or credit cards as there is too much repetition of the same digits and you get confused. I will explain a more robust number system for long strings of digits in Chapter Five.

Rhymes and shapes are fine for three-, four- or five-digit codes. These can include door access codes, PINs, hotel room numbers, year dates or even locations in multi-storey car parks. Take care to include an image or setting that identifies what the number is for. If you have two credit cards, you have to distinguish which PIN goes with which card. Here are some examples:

Your office door access code in 29180.

Imagine the entrance to your office. There is a swan blocking your way. It picks up a tennis racket in its beak and threatens you with it. You light a candle to try and ward it off. It works but the flame from the candle starts to melt a snowman that has a football for a head.

Your Lloyds Bank credit card PIN is 9386.

A black horse has been drinking wine. Intoxicated, it bumps into a tree. The tree topples over, smashing a gate into sticks.

Your hotel room number is 704.

Imagine that your room is adorned with pearly gates like the entrance to heaven. Instead of Saint Peter, Superman (hero) is standing outside and opens the door for you.

The Battle of Bosworth (a significant battle in the Wars of the Roses in which Richard III of York was killed) was in 1485.

Imagine Shakespeare's depiction of Richard III as a hunchbacked villain. As he lies dying on Bosworth Field, he is clutching a candle to illuminate a model sailboat. The boat is captained by a snowman with a pirate hook for a hand.

Your car is parked in the blue zone on level 6.

Imagine a blue elephant standing on the roof of your car.

A word of warning: it may seem trivial to employ a system for a four-digit number but this can be dangerous.

Several years ago I was issued with a new bankcard. I was sent the new PIN in the secure envelope. It was a very simple number – one digit followed by the same digit repeated three times. I thought there was no point in using a system for this and destroyed the slip of paper with the PIN as requested. About a week later I went to a bank cash point. I knew the number was in the format 'xyyy' but I couldn't remember the actual digits. I had to swallow my pride and go into the bank to request a new PIN.

Exercises

Try to come up with imaginative scenes to remember the following:

Sainsbury's Credit Card PIN: 9032

Briefcase combination: 128-540

International Dialling Code for Fiji: + 679

Year of the Battle of Trafalgar: 1805

Summary

- To memorize foreign vocabulary take an object that symbolizes the sound of the word and link it to an object representing the meaning, then make up an imaginative scene.

- To memorize the gender of a word there are three methods:

- Modify your imagined scenes to include masculine or feminine characteristics.

- Allocate 'zones' for masculine and feminine and locate your imagined scenes appropriately.

- Apply 'rules of thumb' to deduce gender.

• The same general principles can be used for English vocabulary and technical terminology.

• You can memorize a list by creating a series of pegs and linking each item in turn to each peg. Pegging is stronger than a series of links in a story, as forgetting one item does not affect the remaining data. It also allows you to come back and fill in any gaps later.

• Peg Systems include:

- Parts of the body

- Numbers via rhymes

- Numbers via shapes

• You can memorize a to-do list on a rolling basis by using a different sequence of pegs on alternate days.

• You can use the number associations in combination with the Link System to memorize short sequences of numbers. Applications include PIN codes, hotel room numbers, door access systems, combination locks and dates.

4:

HOW TO MEMORIZE SPEECHES

In this chapter, I explain a sophisticated form of the Peg System, using physical locations to store information. I show how this can be used for making speeches without notes and how knowledge of memory techniques can help make your message stick with an audience. Finally, I explore some of the history of the technique and its validation by modern brain-scanning technology.

Using Loci

Whenever we experience things in real life they have the context of a location. Often, if you return to the place where something happened, the memories come flooding back. When you create an imagined experience it makes sense to use location.

We have seen that the Link System has no limits in terms of the amount of data that can be connected together but it lacks stability. If a link in the chain of associations is broken, you tend to lose all following items. Peg Systems are much more robust, but limit you to about twenty or so items in a list. The 'Method of Loci', also known as a 'Mental Journey' or 'Memory Palace', gives you the best of both worlds. It helps you to create strong memories with no limits on the amount of data. Loci is the plural of the Latin *locus*, meaning place or location.

The Method of Loci is deceptively simple but very powerful. Imagine taking a tour of your house. You may choose to start your journey in the kitchen. You can walk around noticing the fridge, cupboards, bin, oven and sink. You exit the kitchen into the living room. Once again going round the room you come to the TV, sofa, window, table, fireplace, etc. You reach each object in a specific order. These can be used as pegs. If you have a list of items to remember, associate the first with the fridge, the second leaping out of a cupboard, the third in the bin, and so on. Use the SEA-HORSE principles to make strong, imaginative, active links. To recall the information just retrace your steps, noticing the objects placed or interacting at each location.

Say you have seven rooms in your house. For example, kitchen, living room, stairs and landing, bedroom one, bedroom two, bathroom and garage. If you only select five objects in each, you can remember a list of thirty-five items in order. Of course, you can go into more detail in each room to include ornaments, curtains, even light switches.

You don't have to stop there. You can go outside. Any journey has a series of landmarks that you come across in a set order. These can be trees, shops, post boxes, bus shelters and the like. Take your trip to work, a favourite walk, your childhood home or a holiday destination. The possibilities are almost endless. If you wish, you can create a fantasy route in your ideal house or landscape. I prefer real locations as I think they have greater solidity and less scope for skipping stages along the way. I know one memory athlete who likes to use scenes from favourite films, and Dominic O'Brien, eight times World Memory Champion, sometimes uses golf courses. Experiment with what works best for you. Take care to make each location distinctive. Don't use two windows unless one is a curved bay window and the other is a casement and you can easily distinguish them.

You can use this method to memorize almost any information in sequence. Memory competitors use it for playing cards, lists of words, and random numbers but a really useful application is for making a speech.

Public speaking

In 1984 the *New York Times* performed a survey on Social Anxiety.[14] When people were asked what they most feared, the top two answers were walking into a room full of strangers and speaking in public. Death was rated third!

Why does making a speech feel like a fate worse than death to many people? I think there are two main factors. Firstly, the fear of saying something foolish, and secondly, the fear of forgetting what to say, or 'drying' as actors call it. Presenters with no knowledge of mnemonics employ various tactics. Some read verbatim from a typed script or mobile device. This removes any spontaneity or eye contact with the audience. The presenter is either rooted to the spot behind a lectern or, if able to move, can't make hand gestures as they are holding the script. Worse than this are those who choose to read from a PowerPoint presentation. I am not denigrating the product itself, just the misuse of it. In warfare bullets are fired to kill your enemies. In corporate life bullet points in presentations metaphorically kill your colleagues. Hence the phrase 'death by Power-Point'. I have seen so many awful presentations over the years. One speaker reading their presentation from small text on a screen went so far as to say, 'You probably can't see this.' This was true but if he realized this, what was the point of showing it? Visual aids should not be a substitute for memory and are supposed to aid the audience.

When I worked as a computer programmer for a major bank we had monthly 'cascade meetings'. Someone on the board of the bank, who we'd never met, had one of his staff create a PowerPoint presentation. This was given to the senior managers, each of whom then presented it to their subordinates, so the information from the top cascaded though the organization. This is fine, in principle. In practice, it was torture. Nobody wanted to be in the meeting, least of all the manager giving the presentation. He would read from the screen displaying no personality or interest while everyone else tried to look awake. It was a massive waste of time, resulting in loss of productivity. If the text had been circulated by email, it could have been read in a fraction of the time taken to present it. You couldn't guarantee that everyone would read it, but given the way it was presented, you could be sure nobody would remember the content anyway.

The best presenters use PowerPoint to display mostly pictures, clear diagrams, Mind Maps, animations and – very occasionally – sparse keywords. They never show dense text or bullet-point lists. Video clips can sometimes be effective. Keep them very short and don't try to talk over them. Stand to one side, let the audience watch and then elaborate or discuss.

Always speak without notes. When you do so the audience perceives you as more honest and truthful, something politicians realize. Max Atkinson, one of Britain's leading public speaking coaches, says, 'The autocue allows the speaker to simulate continuous eye contact, but it has become a bit obvious. Speaking without notes goes further; the audience will feel you're speaking from the heart, which is what you want. In any event, it's raising the bar.'[15]

The ability to memorize the content of a presentation and speak without notes has many practical benefits. It allows you to connect with the audience, thus building rapport. This is achieved through eye contact, use of congruent gestures, relaxed delivery and the freedom to use the whole stage.

You can choose to memorize a script word-for-word or just memorize the outline of what you want to cover. You may decide on a combination of the two, committing some stories to memory in detail whilst allowing more freedom with descriptions or theories.

As you are not necessarily slavishly following a script you have the opportunity to express your personality, to genuinely converse with the audience, and, if appropriate, to answer questions or share jokes. You can be more flexible so if you have less time than anticipated you can choose to skip sections without any fear of losing your thread. If you have extra time, you can easily elaborate on certain topics. Any fear is dramatically reduced as you know that you know your material. You may still have some butterflies in your stomach but they can be marshalled to fly in formation!

One word of warning: make sure of your memory system before walking on stage. Allow time for rehearsal and to reinforce any areas where you are less certain of the links. Former leader of the Labour Party Ed Miliband famously forgot the sections on reducing the UK budget deficit and immigration in a speech at the party conference in Manchester in September 2014. Asked on ITV1's *Good Morning Britain* whether he had forgotten them, he said: 'Absolutely, yes. It's not really about memorizing the speech. What I try and do is write a speech and then I use it as the basis for what I want to say to the country.'[16]

Writing a memorable speech

An understanding of how memory works not only helps you as a presenter, but can also be used to help your audience remember the important points you want to make.

Opening and closing

Early twentieth-century psychologist Hermann Ebbinghaus performed experiments on himself to determine the nature of recall and forgetting. One of his major findings is called the 'serial position effect',[17] also known as 'recall during learning'. This states that in any period of study, such as listening to a speech or lecture, the accuracy of recall varies according to the position of information in the presentation. On average people remember content from the beginning, known as the 'primacy effect' and, to a slightly lesser extent, things from near the end, known as the 'recency effect'. Relatively little is recalled from the middle.

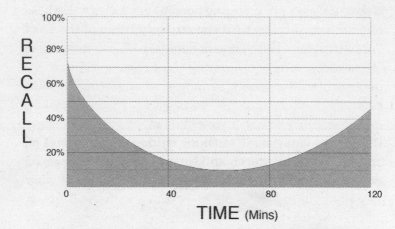

To help your audience remember your key points it makes sense to state them at the beginning and summarize again at the end. This was expounded by self-improvement lecturer Dale Carnegie when he said, 'Tell them what you are going to tell them; tell them; tell them what you have told them.' This is sometimes criticized by professional speakers and often misunderstood. Carnegie was not expounding mindless repetition. He was explaining the idea of setting the scene and signposting where the talk is going at the beginning. This helps the audience buy in to what you're about to say. In the middle you go into the detail (I'll explain more about this shortly). At the end, summarize with an engaging, motivational closing.

This is how TV news programmes are structured. They start with 'the headlines tonight'. This is followed by a summary of the stories with reports from correspondents, discussion, interviews and comments in the studio. The programme ends with 'a reminder of tonight's top stories' and sometimes a heart-warming or funny 'and finally' piece. Make sure you have engaging openings and closings. These are worth perfecting and memorizing verbatim.

We will learn much more about Ebbinghaus's research in Chapter Nine.

The middle bit

Think back to the SEAHORSE principles explained in Chapter Two. Tell stories to keep your audience engaged and able to remember points from the middle of your presentation. These should be personal with good use of sensual descriptions – active, humorous and emotionally involving. Make use of the Von Restorff Effect. Anything different or unexpected will stand out in the audience members' minds.

The rule of three

The brain likes to find patterns. Two items can hint at a pattern but a third confirms it. Lists of three related items are very memorable. This fact is often used to good effect by politicians and advertisers. Think of the following:

'Friends, Romans, Countrymen, lend me your ears'
William Shakespeare

'Our priorities are education, education, education'
Tony Blair

'A Mars a day helps you work, rest and play'
Advertising slogan created by Francis Harmar Brown

'Never in the field of human conflict was so much owed by so many to so few' *Winston Churchill*

The same rule underpins many jokes. The first two items set up a pattern and the third breaks it. My apologies in advance for lack of political correctness.

An Englishman, a Frenchman and an Irishman were in a pub talking about their children.

'My son was born on St George's Day,' remarked the Englishman, 'so we obviously decided to call him George.'

'That's a real coincidence,' observed the Frenchman. 'My daughter was born on Valentine's Day, so we decided to call her Valentine.'

'That's incredible,' exclaimed the Irishman. 'Exactly the same thing happened with my son Pancake.'

The format can even be the butt of the joke.

A priest, a minister and a rabbi walk into a bar. The bartender looks at them and says, 'What is this, a joke?'

Memorizing your speech

1. Break into key words Take your script or outline of your presentation and, depending on the level of detail you need to memorize, break it into key words.

2. Create images from the key words and link them Select or create a journey with the corresponding numbers or locations. Using an image to symbolize each key word, populate your journey. Make your associations as vivid, playful and unusual as possible. If you can have the items interacting with the locations, so much the better.

3. Review and refine the image journey Review the journey and refine any associations that are indistinct.

If you can gain access to the auditorium where you will be speaking ahead of time, it is a really great idea to use real locations in the room as stages of your journey. During your speech you can glance around the room being reminded of your key points. To your audience you just seem to be making eye contact and acting entirely naturally. They will be immensely impressed at your seemingly off-the-cuff erudition.

A brief history of Loci

This technique is very old. It dates back more than two thousand years. The Ancient Greeks used to write on papyrus, parchment from animal skins, and wax tablets. However, these were precious commodities – certainly not to be used to scribble notes for a speech that would later be thrown away. For this reason, the orators of the time had to rely on their memory to speak and debate.

According to legend the Method of Loci was discovered by Greek poet Simonides of Ceos. Whilst attending a banquet at the house of a wealthy nobleman named Scopas, Simonides recited a poem he had composed in honour of the host. The poem also praised the twin mythological sons of Leda, Castor and Pollux, patrons of travellers and of sailors. This displeased Scopas who insisted that he would only pay half of the fee agreed for the poem and Simonides could ask the gods for the balance. A short while later a message was passed to Simonides informing him that there were two men who were insistent he should go out to meet them. On leaving the banqueting hall he saw no one but as soon as he stepped outside the building it collapsed, killing all the other guests. It would seem that the gods had paid their debt. The bodies were so badly mutilated in the disaster that they could not be identified. Simonides was able to direct relatives accordingly by recalling the position where each guest was seated. This led him to the realization that location is an important tool for committing information to memory.

Knowledge of memory techniques was later adopted by the Romans. Quintilian was a Roman orator and teacher of rhetoric (c.35–c.100 CE). In his twelve-volume textbook on the subject, *Institutio Oratoria,* he writes the following on the Method of Loci:

> The first thought is placed, as it were, in the forecourt; the second, let us say, in the living room; the remainder are placed in due order all round the impluvium[*] and entrusted not merely to bedrooms and parlours, but

---

[*] Impluvium, n. (in an ancient Roman building), a pool under an opening in the roof.

even to the care of statues and the like. This done, as soon as the memory of the facts requires to be revived, all these places are visited in turn and the various deposits are demanded from their custodians, as the sight of each recalls the respective details. Consequently, however large the number of these which it is required to remember, all are linked one to the other like dancers hand in hand, and there can be no mistake what precedes to what follows, no trouble being required except the preliminary labour of committing the various points to memory.

What I have spoken of as being done in a house, can equally well be done in connexion with public buildings, a long journey, the ramparts of a city, or even pictures. Or we may even imagine such places to ourselves. We require, therefore, places, real or imaginary, and images or symbols, which we must, of course, invent for ourselves. By images I mean the words by which we distinguish the things which we have to learn by heart: in fact, as Cicero says, we use 'places like wax tablets and symbols in lieu of letters'.

Recent research

In 2002 the Institute of Neurology in London conducted Functional Magnetic Resonance Imaging (fMRI) on ten top memorizers.[18] The results indicated that their brains were no different to average. However, when memorizing, it was clear that they were activating the hippocampus. We saw in Chapter Two that this has a role in the consolidation of information from short-term to long-term memory and in spatial navigation. It makes sense that, since the memorizers were using mental journeys, the navigational circuits of their brains were activated.

Having seen how we can memorize long lists of information using the Method of Loci, we need to put this to use. The key factor is how we symbolize or encode information in a form suitable to put in locations. In the next chapter, we consider this in the context of numbers.

Summary

- You can use a series of locations along a journey, internally or externally, to act as memory pegs.

- The Method of Loci can be used to memorize any data in sequence but is especially beneficial for delivering a speech from memory without the need for notes.

- Break the presentation into keywords. Place an image for each point in turn at each location along the journey. Make your association as vivid and strong as possible.

- Remember to give yourself time to rehearse to strengthen the memory.

- To recall the information simply retrace your steps, noticing the object at each location.

- When designing a presentation follow the following principles:

    - A clear introduction signposting where the talk is going

- Unusual elements, repetition and engaging stories in the middle of the speech

- An inspiring and powerful ending

- Use groups of three elements when you need to emphasize an important point

• The technique dates back to Ancient Greece and Rome but is supported by modern brain-imaging technology.

5:

HOW TO MEMORIZE NUMBERS

We encounter long numbers in many areas of our lives, from national insurance numbers to passport numbers, credit card numbers, bank account numbers and phone numbers. Our inability to memorize large numbers has spawned a vast array of technological solutions. Your mobile phone stores all the numbers you need. Your computer can store your credit card number. You may have a PayPal account that links to your bank so that you can pay online in a single click. We will talk about Internet security and passwords in Chapter Seven. What happens if your phone gets stolen or lost? Do you back up all your data regularly?

Are we getting lazier?

Technology, whilst making our lives easier, is making our brains lazier. If you go everywhere in your car and never take any exercise, your body will get fat and slow. The brain is no different. It is like a muscle that needs to be stimulated and exercised. Research at the University of Waterloo, Canada,[19] states, 'That people typically forego effortful analytic thinking in lieu of fast and easy intuition suggests that individuals may allow their Smartphones to do their thinking for them.' It concludes, 'These findings demonstrate that people may offload thinking to technology, which in turn demands that psychological science understand the meshing of mind and media to adequately characterize human experience and cognition in the modern era.' It is very dangerous to abdicate use of your memory and hence thinking.

Possibly concerned with people's inability to remember phone numbers, BT's website offers '*25 simple ways to boost your brain and improve your memory*'. These include chewing gum, eating berries, doing yoga and climbing trees. Interestingly, they didn't think to include learning memory techniques in their list!

In this chapter I will explain a far better strategy for memorizing numbers. It builds on the techniques we have already covered and makes numbers of any length manageable.

Why do we need a new system?

In Chapter Three I introduced you to the Number Rhyme and Number Shape Systems. These convert the abstract concept of numbers into concrete objects that you can visualize, and associate together. Both systems have the advantage of simplicity but a disadvantage – if you try to memorize a long number, the same objects crop up time and time again. If you're imagining a story with three snowmen representing 'eights' and four swans representing 'twos', for instance, it is very easy to get confused. The 'Major System' for numbers largely overcomes this problem, although it requires slightly more preparation to use.

The Major System

It is relatively easy to memorize a list of nouns using the Link System, the Peg System or the Method of Loci. The Major System aims to convert numbers into letters and build words that can then be memorized in the normal way by symbolizing them with images and making associations.

Have you played the game Scrabble? The aim is to make up words using combinations of lettered tiles, each with a points value. Letters that are more commonly found in English words such as 'T' have fewer points than those more rarely used like 'X', 'J' or 'Z'.

> 1 point – A, E, I, O, U, L, N, S, T, R
> 2 points – D, G
> 3 points – B, C, M, P
> 4 points – F, H, V, W, Y
> 5 points – K
> 8 points – J, X
> 10 points – Q, Z

To make it easier to come up with words, the Major System assigns letter sounds to numbers using mainly the 'lower' value Scrabble tiles.

Codify to simplify

Numbers are represented by the following phonetic code. Spelling is not important, as the Major System is simply based on sounds. This may seem a little random at first but stay with me and it'll make sense.

0 = 's' or soft 'c' as in 'sauce' (the first sound of the word 'zero')

1 = 'd' or 't' (both have one down stroke when written in lower case)

2 = 'n' (this has two down strokes)

3 = 'm' (three down strokes)

4 = 'r' (the fourth letter of the word 'four')

5 = 'l' (if you hold out the five digits of your hand, they make an 'L' shape)

6 = 'sh' or soft 'g' as in 'rage' (the letter 'g' and '6' are similar shapes when rotated)

7 = hard 'c' as in 'cake', a hard 'g' as in 'nag' or 'k' (if you rotate two number sevens, they can make a 'K' shape)

8 = 'f' or 'v' as in 'lava' (a handwritten 'f' has two loops like a number eight)

9 = 'b' or 'p' (if you write a nine with a straight vertical, then 'b' and 'p' are similar shapes when reflected or rotated)

Take digits in pairs, convert into letter sounds with the above code and create a word by adding vowels that carry no value.

For example '42' yields 'R' and 'N' so you can make 'RaiN'.

Once you have learned the code you can make up words and thus images as you go through a number. For example, the first 10 digits of the number π are 3.141592653.

31 = m t = mat
41 = r t = rat
59 = l b = lab
26 = n sh = nosh
53 = l m = lamb

Imagine a welcome mat placed outside a chemistry classroom in your old school. A large rat wearing a white coat scuttles in and demonstrates a lab experiment. After finishing he enjoys sharing a bowl of nosh with a baby lamb.

Making conversions 'on the fly' like this can be time consuming. You can speed up the process by preparing a standard set of 100 words representing the numbers from 00 to 99. These have to be pre-learned but once you know them you can memorize numbers very quickly. I recommend that you come up with your own associations as these will be more immediate and easier to recall. Fill in the grid opposite before reading on.

If you get stuck, you can use some of the associations on page 78 adapted from a list compiled by Dr Sue Whiting,[20] former Women's World Memory Champion. In most instances the selected word is the one that would appear first in a dictionary. For example, 11 is 'date' rather than 'teddy'.

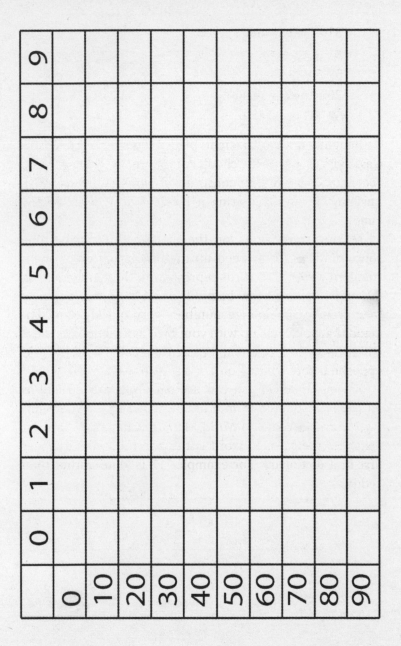

	0	1	2	3	4	5	6	7	8	9
0										
10										
20										
30										
40										
50										
60										
70										
80										
90										

	0	1	2	3	4	5	6	7	8	9
0	Sauce	Soot	Sun	Sum	Saw	Sail	Sash	Sack	Sofa	Soap
10	Daisy	Date	Dine	Dam	Door	Deal	Dish	Duck	Dive	Dopey
20	NASA	Net	Nan	Name	Nar(whal)	Nail	Niche	Nag	Navy	Nab
30	Maze	Mat	Man	Ma'am	Mare	Mail	Mash	Mac	Mafia	Map
40	Race	Rat	Rain	Ram	Ra-Ra	Rail	Rage	Rack	Raffia	Rap
50	Lace	Lad	Lane	Lamb	Lair	Lily	Lash	Lake	Lava	Lab
60	Chase	Chat	Chain	Chime	Chair	Cello	Cha-Cha	Cheque	Chaff	Chap
70	Case	Cat	Can	Cameo	Car	Call	Cash	Cake	Café	Cab
80	Face	Fad	Fan	Fame	Fair	Fall	Fish	Fag	Fife	Fab
90	Base	Bat	Ban	Bam	Bar	Ball	Bash	Book	Beef	Babe

Alternative number-to-letter code systems

Variations on this theme have been used by many memory champions to memorize thousands of digits in competitions. Their innovations were to employ certain 'data compression' methods to reduce the number of Loci required. Here are three such techniques.

Dominic O'Brien (Person, Action)

This system uses a simpler code mainly based on a number's position in the alphabet:

$$0 = o \text{ (similar shape)}$$
$$1 = a$$
$$2 = b$$
$$3 = c$$
$$4 = d$$
$$5 = e$$
$$6 = s \text{ (six has an 's' sound)}$$
$$7 = g$$
$$8 = h$$
$$9 = n \text{ (nine has an 'n' sound)}$$

Rather than making up words Dominic uses his letters as the initials of people's names. For example, 15 = AE = Albert Einstein.

To save on the number of Loci required for a long number, Dominic adds a second step to the process. He imagines an action that each character would typically do. Albert Einstein could be found chalking equations on a blackboard.

Dominic takes the first pair of digits and converts them

into a person. He then has this person performing the action that is associated with the second pair. For example, 18 = AH = Adolf Hitler. So the number 1815 (the date of the Battle of Waterloo) becomes Adolf Hitler chalking on a blackboard. Thus a single image represents 4 digits.

Andy Bell (Person, Action, Object)

This system takes the process one step further. Each two-digit number is allocated a person, an action and an object. These are then combined to give six digits per location. For example, the number 203542 encodes as:

> 20 = BO = Barack Obama (Person)
>
> 35 = CE = Clint Eastwood (Action – lassoing)
>
> 42 = DB = David Beckham (Object – a football)

Barack Obama lassoing a football.

Ben Pridmore (Extended Major System)

Ben takes groups of three digits and uses the standard Major System code, on page 75, to convert the first and third digit into consonant sounds. His adaptation is to use the system below to code the middle digit into a specific vowel.

> 0 = 'oo' as in 'you'
>
> 1 = 'a' as in 'cat'
>
> 2 = 'e' as in 'pet'
>
> 3 = 'i' as in 'kitten'
>
> 4 = 'o' as in 'tom'
>
> 5 = 'u' as in 'puss'
>
> 6 = 'A' as in 'hay'
>
> 7 = 'E' as in 'bee'

8 = 'I' as in 'high'

9 = 'O' as in 'low'

For example, 974 = bEr = beer, 901 = boot, etc.

Some of his associations are people and others are objects, but this has no significance in his system.

For compactness, Ben places three associated objects/people per location arranged arbitrarily from left to right, or top to bottom.

This gives nine digits per location.

Whilst the Person/Action system requires you to pre-learn 200 associations and the Person/Action/Object needs 300, Ben's system requires 1,000. Despite allowing fast memorization of large volumes of data it requires a lot of dedication to implement, so it is probably too much work unless you want to enter memory competitions.

The history of the Major System

It is probable that the system was named after Bartlomiej Beniowski, a major in the Polish lancers. His system was published in 1845 but the technique dates back long before this.

The first recorded instance of converting numbers into consonants to aid memory seems to be the Ancient Indian Katapayadi system, from circa 683 CE, introduced by the astronomer-mathematician Haridatta.

The early origins of the system we know today date back to Pierre Hérigone (1580–1643), a French mathematician and astronomer. This was further developed by Stanislaus Mink von Wennsshein and published in 1648.

Richard Grey created a system that used both consonants and vowels in 1730 which is remarkably similar to Ben Pridmore's modern system. In 1808 Gregor von Feinaigle (1760–1819), a German mnemonist and Roman Catholic monk, introduced the notion of representing the digits by consonant sounds. French scholar Aimé Paris (1798–1866) modified Gregor von Feinaigle's system to create what we know as the modern Major System. Francis Fauvel-Gouraud (1808–47) was a French pioneer in photography and became Thomas Edison's agent in London as well as an expert mnemonist. He published Aimé Paris's version of the modern Major System in his book *Phreno-Mnemotechny* or *The Art of Memory* (Houel and Macoy, 1844).

In recent times the system has been popularized by the American magician, writer and memory-training specialist Harry Lorayne and English author and educational consultant Tony Buzan.

Buzan recounts how he was first introduced to the system by his English professor[20]. Professor Clark was renowned for his genius and his dislike of students. At Tony's first class at university, Clark deliberately arrived late and called the class roll from memory. Whenever he encountered an absent student on the list he would recite their address, phone number, date of birth and parents' names, all without reference to notes. 'When he had completed the roll call with "Zygotski?" . . . "Here, sir!", he looked at the students sardonically and said, with a droll smile, "That means Cartland, Chapman, Harkstone, Hughes, Luxmore, Mears and Tovey are absent!" He paused again, and then said: "I'll make a note of that . . . sometime!" So saying, he turned and left the room in stunned silence.'

Memorizing budgets and statistics

You can use the Major System to relatively easily memorize financial information and statistics. The table below shows departmental expenditure limits (DEL) for UK government departments over previous years produced by HM Treasury and the Office for National Statistics. Of course, the same technique can be used for a company balance sheet, your personal finances or any other table of figures.

Let's just look at the more recent figures in the right-hand column. I will demonstrate the first ten rows. In each case we create a location representing the department and then link the images representing the numbers.

Education 50,902

50 = lace

90 = base

2 = swan (number shape)

Table 6 Resource DEL excluding depreciation, 2009-10 to 2013-14

	2009-10 outturn	2010-11 outturn	2011-12 outturn	2012-13 outturn	£ million 2013-14 outturn
Resource DEL excluding depreciation by departmental group					
Education	49,247	50,349	50,122	49,977	50,902
NHS (Health)	93,237	96,260	99,073	101,440	105,424
Personal Social Services (Health) [1]	1,362	1,471	-	-	-
Transport	5,652	5,176	4,679	4,315	3,784
CLG Communities	4,299	3,799	1,914	1,455	2,051
CLG Local Government [2]	26,804	24,402	25,388	23,188	16,481
Business, Innovation and Skills	17,296	17,010	16,208	15,443	14,861
Home Office	9,271	12,292	11,908	11,143	10,722
Justice	8,664	8,723	8,589	8,201	7,521
Law Officers' Departments	697	658	611	591	565
Defence	27,587	28,090	28,142	26,415	26,968
Foreign and Commonwealth Office	2,022	2,097	2,052	1,989	1,998
International Development	5,234	5,909	6,167	6,105	8,074
Energy and Climate Change	1,219	1,149	1,147	1,120	1,165
Environment, Food and Rural Affairs	2,256	2,169	1,982	1,860	1,749
Culture, Media and Sport	1,461	1,475	1,504	2,093	1,094
Work and Pensions	13,414	13,782	12,247	12,122	7,432
Scotland	24,487	25,211	24,814	24,968	25,466
Wales	13,072	13,382	13,232	13,248	13,709
Northern Ireland	9,302	9,605	9,443	9,464	9,724
Chancellor's Departments	4,035	3,745	3,628	3,235	3,152
Cabinet Office	1,962	2,025	2,045	2,147	2,108
Small and Independent Bodies	1,610	1,569	1,645	1,406	1,476
Total resource DEL excluding depreciation	**324,191**	**330,347**	**326,540**	**321,925**	**316,427**

Imagine a classroom where a teacher dressed in a frilly lace blouse pitches a baseball to a swan holding a bat in its beak.

NHS 105,424

10 = daisy

54 = lyre

24 = narwhal (a single-tusked arctic whale)

In a hospital ward imagine daisy chains draped around a bed where a nurse plays a lyre to sooth a narwhal patient to sleep.

Transport 3,784

37 = mac

84 = fair

In a bus station a man in a mac is riding on a fairground carousel that has been erected.

Communities and Local Government – Communities 2,051

20 = NASA

51 = lad

In a community centre there is a NASA space capsule from which a young lad disembarks.

Communities and Local Government – Local Government 16,481

16 = dish

48 = raffia

1 = candle (number shape)

Outside the council offices a large dish is placed on a raffia tablemat and then a candle is lit beside it for a romantic meal.

Business, Innovation and Skills 14,861

14 = door

86 = fish

1 = candle (number shape)

You open a big heavy oak-panelled door to go into the boardroom of a corporation. Flapping about on the long table is a big fish. As it swishes its tail it knocks a candle onto the floor.

Home Office 10,722

10 = daisy

72 = can

2 = swan (number shape)

I would imagine this scene taking place in my office at home. If you don't have an office, imagine your living room. The floor is covered in a carpet of daisies. You decide to open a can of weed-killer but a swan swoops in and grabs it out of your hand.

Justice 7,521

75 = call

21 = net

In a courtroom a phone is ringing but instead of answering the call it is dropped into a net to be removed so as not to disturb the proceedings.

Law Officers' Departments 565

56 = lash

5 = hook (number shape)

In a police station imagine a woman police officer having mascara applied to her eye lashes by Captain Hook.

Defence 26,968

26 = niche

96 = bash

8 = snowman (number shape)

On a WWI battlefield a soldier takes a big stick from a niche in a wall of a trench and uses it to bash a snowman to pieces. He claims it is in self-defence.

You can complete the remainder for practice.

Remembering dates, birthdays and anniversaries

Many people find it a challenge to remember birthdays and anniversaries. Of course, technology or even old-fashioned paper calendars can help with this but it is much better mental exercise to memorize important dates. Donald Trump tried to praise the heroes of 9/11 at a Buffalo rally on 18th April 2016 but spoilt the compliment by saying police and fire fighters responded on 7-Eleven. It was clearly a slip of the tongue and he didn't really get the World Trade Center attack and a convenience store chain confused in

Mind Map of Chapter 1: Linguistic memory systems

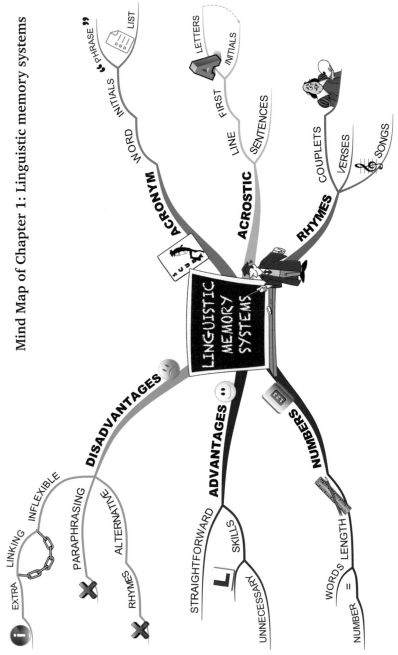

Mind Map of Chapter 2: Enhanced memory systems

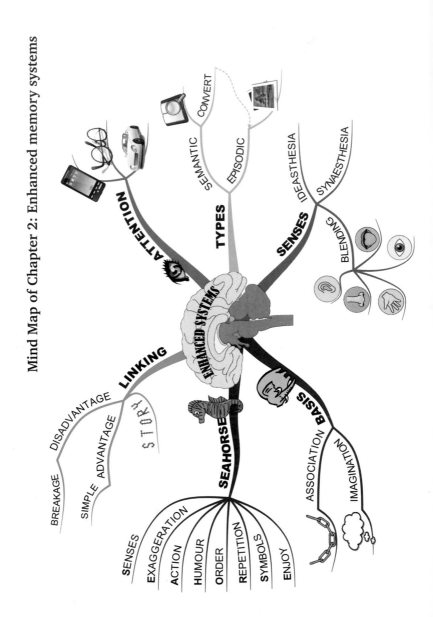

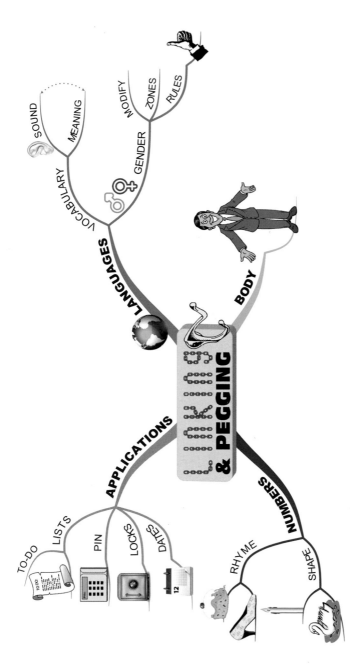

Mind Map of Chapter 3: Linking and pegging skills

Mind Map of Chapter 4: How to memorize speeches

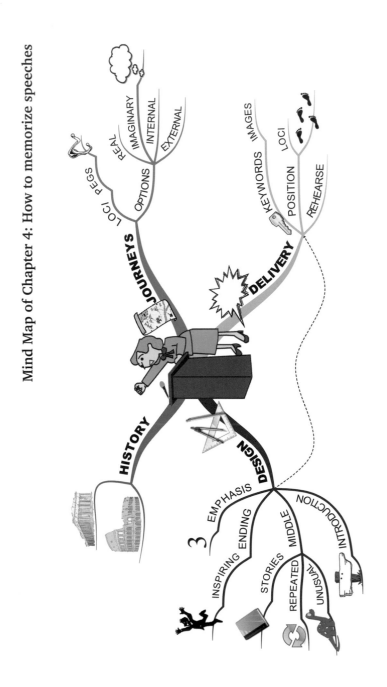

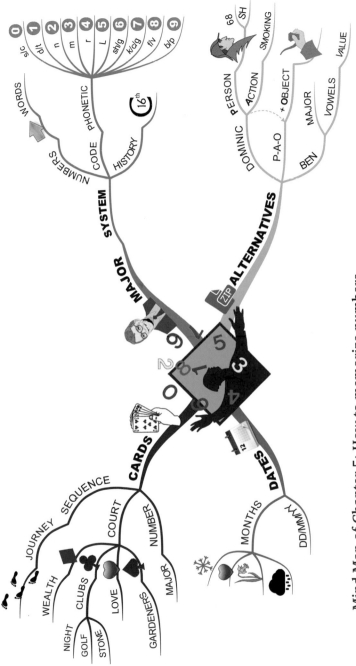

Mind Map of Chapter 5: How to memorize numbers

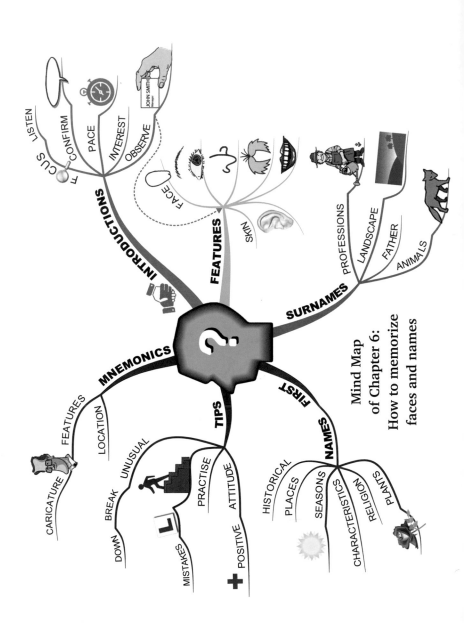

Mind Map
of Chapter 6:
How to memorize
faces and names

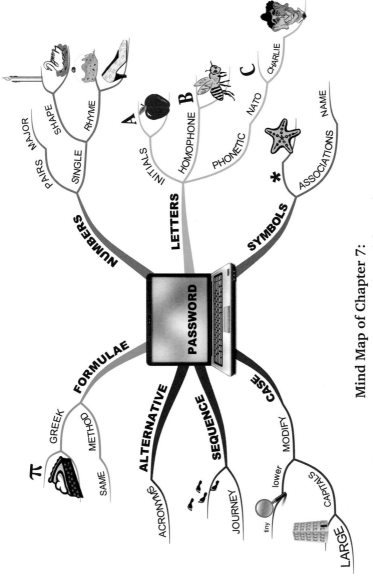

Mind Map of Chapter 7:
How to memorize passwords and formulae

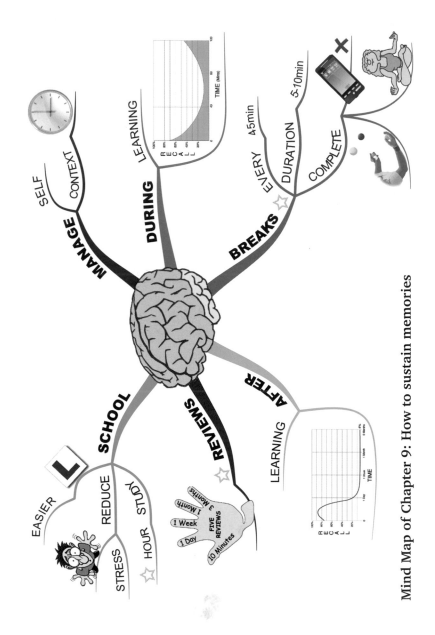

Mind Map of Chapter 9: How to sustain memories

his mind, but he should have been more mindful of his dates.

To memorize a date you can simply convert it into a six-digit number in the format DD/MM/YY and use the Major System to associate images with the event or person to whom the date relates. For example, Queen Elizabeth II was born on 21/04/26, which equates to Net, Saw, Niche. Perhaps the Queen drops her crown. She scoops it up in a butterfly net, saws off the handle and then puts it securely into a niche in the palace.

An alternative is to create a standard set of twelve objects to represent the months and just use the Major System for day and year. This has the advantage that you can't get confused as to whether a date is in American format with the month first or UK format with the day first.

> January – snowflake
>
> February – heart (for Valentine's Day)
>
> March – daffodil (for St. David's Day)
>
> April – rain showers or a jester (for April Fool's Day)
>
> May – maypole
>
> June – Stonehenge (for the Summer Solstice)
>
> July – Statue of Liberty (for American Independence Day)
>
> August – Augustus Caesar
>
> September – autumn leaves
>
> October – pumpkin (for Halloween)
>
> November – fireworks (from Guy Fawkes Night)
>
> December – Christmas tree

For example, staying on the royal theme, Prince William, Duke of Cambridge, was born on 21 June 1982. Incidentally, I find this easy to remember as my birthday is also 21 June.

Net (for 21), Stonehenge (for June) and a fan (for 82).

Prince William grabs a net and races round Stonehenge trying to catch a royal fan.

Practice exercise

Try to memorize the following data using the Major System and either a journey or a simple Link System. They are real numbers (apart from the credit card).

Mastercard Credit Card:
5536 7439 7778 0091

Phone number of Shrewsbury Town Football Club:
01743 289177

Phone number of King's Cross Station Lost Property Office (a number you should never need with a trained memory!):
0330 024 0215

ISBN for *The Student Survival Guide* by Phil Chambers and Elaine Colliar:
978 1 904906 03 2

Approximate value of mathematical constant e, the base of natural logarithms. (Compare with the

sentence method used in Chapter One.):
2.7182818284590

Memorizing playing cards

Memorizing the order of a shuffled deck of fifty-two cards is the ultimate card trick. Of course, it is not a trick but an application of a number system. You already have most of the component parts to achieve this amazing feat.

Each of the number cards can be converted into a Major System word. Take the number of the card as the first syllable and the suit as the second. Use one for ace and zero for ten. Spades is 'S', diamonds is 'D/T', clubs is 'C' and since we don't have an 'H' in the system use 'SH' for hearts.

Ace of Spades = daisy
Two of Spades = NASA
Three of Spades = maze
Four of Spades = race
Five of Spades = lace
Six of Spades = chase
Seven of Spades = case
Eight of Spades = face
Nine of Spades = base (ball)
Ten of Spades = sauce

Ace of Diamonds = date
Two of Diamonds = net
Three of Diamonds = mat
Four of Diamonds = rat
Five of Diamonds = lad
Six of Diamonds = chat

Seven of Diamonds = cat
Eight of Diamonds = fad
Nine of Diamonds = bat
Ten of Diamonds = soot

Similarly for Clubs and Hearts.

As court cards are people it makes sense to represent them with associated people. You could choose a theme for each suit:

Diamonds with wealth:
King of Diamonds – Bill Gates
Queen of Diamonds – Queen Elizabeth II
Jack of Diamonds – Richard Branson

Spades with gardening:
King of Spades – Alan Tichmarsh
Queen of Spades – Charlie Dimmock
Jack of Spades – Monty Don

Hearts with sex symbols or love:
King of Hearts – George Clooney
Queen of Hearts – Angelina Jolie
Jack of Hearts – Brad Pitt

Clubs with night, stone or golf clubs:
King of Clubs – Peter Stringfellow
Queen of Clubs – Wilma Flintstone
Jack of Clubs – Rory McIlroy

Now you have an association with each card you just position them among a fifty-two location journey to give you the order.

Of course, using the data compression techniques described above, you require shorter journeys. In this way

Ben Pridmore was able to memorize twenty-eight decks perfectly in one hour. This record was broken in 2015 by Shi Binbin of China and now stands at thirty-one decks – that's 1,612 cards.

Summary

- The Major System converts numbers into words such that they can be more easily visualized and hence memorized.

- This is accomplished by converting digits to consonant sounds using a code and then making words by padding out with vowels which have no value associated to them.

- It is advisable to create a standard set of associated words from 00 = sauce to 99 = babe.

- Alternative systems exist to 'compress' data and thus allow more digits to be memorized in each location along a journey. These include:

  – Using a code to convert numbers into the initials of people's names and then assigning an action to each person.

  – This can further be extended by creating a person, action and object for each pair of digits.

  – An alternative is to use the Major System code but assign values to vowel sounds.

- The Major System has a long history dating back to the sixteenth century.

- To memorize dates you can either convert them into a six-digit number in the format DD/MM/YY and memorize as above or use an alternative association for the month.

- Playing cards can be memorized as follows:
  - Convert number cards into Major System words.
  - Represent court cards by people.
  - Memorize the order by placing associated images for the words along a fifty-two location journey.

6:

HOW TO MEMORIZE FACES AND NAMES

'A person's name,' according to Dale Carnegie, 'is, to him or her, the sweetest and most important sound in any language.' I don't fully agree with this statement, but names do play a vitally important role in our lives. And the number one question I am asked is how to remember them.

At one time or another, we have all had a conversation with someone – often who we've met before – while having absolutely no idea what their name is. This can be agonizingly embarrassing and we think of tricks to cover up our shortcomings, such as asking the person to introduce him- or herself to someone else, to get a second chance to find out what their name is.

The inability to remember names leads to false terms of endearment being used as a substitute. You may be called 'my dear', 'love', 'sweetheart' or 'darling'. When greeting someone, terms such as 'hello there / you / mate' try to disguise the fact that you've forgotten someone's name.

Some people are so certain that the problem is insurmountable that they brag about having a poor memory. They will say things such as 'I won't remember your name' or 'I never forget a face but I am rubbish at names'. This becomes a self-fulfilling prophecy. If you believe you can't remember names, you stop trying to do so.

The truth is that with the right techniques, names, like any other data, can be committed to memory. In this chapter, I will give you some general tips on how to actively focus on facial characteristics and learn more about the origins of names. Finally, we will cover two specific mnemonic techniques, which employ location or facial characteristics to lock a name into your memory.

Look and listen

When being introduced to someone make sure you are focused, attentive and carefully listening. As I mentioned in Chapter Two, if you are focusing on what you are going to say next, you are not registering the name. Little wonder you forget it. Take a genuine interest in the people you meet. If you are unsure that you heard the name correctly, or if it is an unusual name, you can ask the person to repeat or even spell it for you. Try to take control of the pace of introductions. Have a few words with each person you meet. This gives you a chance to consolidate the name in your mind and link it to the person's face.

You may be struck by mannerisms. If you look at impressionists, they are limited by how much they can change their appearance. They have a very close approximation to the voice of the person they're impersonating but the picture is only complete when they mimic or exaggerate mannerisms.

Does the person have a distinctive voice or accent? Think about Stephen Fry, Brian Blessed and Hugh Grant. You can probably imagine and recall their voices almost as well as their appearance.

Face shape and features

Closely observe the features of a person's face. If you look carefully, you will see that there is a huge amount of variation between faces. Imagine you're a detective using a police identikit to build up the picture of a suspect or a portrait painter forming a likeness in your mind.

Does the person have a round or a more elongated face? Is their head large, medium or small compared with their overall body size?

Research into face shape was conducted by Dr Kendra Schmid in Australia.[21] It was commissioned by OPSM Opticians to help advise on the most appropriate glasses frames for a particular shape of face. The study used computer analysis of over 1,000 faces from different states across Australia and identified nine distinct shapes. The *Daily Mail*, Australia, reported the findings:

1. Kite
Characteristics: kite face shapes have prominent cheekbones, which are slightly wider than the mid and lower forehead. The kite face narrows at the jawline and the chin.

2. Heart
Characteristics: heart faces have a longer and wider forehead, with cheekbones a similar width to the lower forehead. Hearts have a slightly more prominent jaw than kite shapes and are narrow at the chin.

3. Rectangle
Characteristics: rectangle faces are recognizable by their defined jawline, and are of similar width to the cheekbone and lower forehead.

4. Oval

Characteristics: ovals are typically smaller than average on all measures. Oval faces are widest at the cheekbone and narrow through the forehead and jaw.

5. Round

Characteristics: round faces have soft, balanced features, typically with a shorter face length and narrower cheek and jawline.

6. Square

Characteristics: an angular face shape, where the forehead and chin lengths are almost equal. Square faces are angular with wider but equal forehead, cheekbone and jaw width.

7. Teardrop

Characteristics: the teardrop is a shorter face, with a narrow forehead and cheekbone. This is the only group for which the forehead length is shorter than the chin.

8. Heptagon

Characteristics: heptagon faces are typically longer than average. Their most striking features are a wide forehead and prominent cheekbones.

9. Oblong

Characteristics: while rare, the oblong differs from other groups by being longer and wider through all measures.

No one particular face shape is regarded as more attractive than the others.

Eyes

'The eyes are the window to your soul,' or so the saying goes. The eyes of a person are certainly one of their most memorable features.

Eye colour varies from pale powder-blue or grey, through deeper shades of blue, green, hazel to deep brown. Neither blue nor green pigments are ever present in the human iris. The perceived colour is a result of light scattering and can change in different lighting conditions. Each person's iris pattern is unique and iris recognition forms part of the biometric 'ePassport' standards.

Eye shapes also show a great deal of variation. They can be deep-set or bulging; close together or far apart; narrow or wide; and sometimes slanting. Look at the area around the eyes. Are there bags under the eyes or 'crow's feet' at the corners? What shape is the eyelid? Observe the eyelashes. Don't be distracted by spectacles.

Eyebrows

Eyebrows can be bushy, thin, arched, flat or pencilled in. They may meet in the middle, forming a monobrow.

Nose

Noses can be large, small, wide, narrow, upturned, flat, straight, Roman, aquiline or snub. Nostrils can be flared, wide, narrow and sometimes untrimmed and hairy.

Hair

Hair, whilst being a very identifiable characteristic, is often dramatically altered according to fashion. Hairstyle and colour can be changed. Men may choose to grow a beard or moustache and could go bald or grey.

Mouth, lips and teeth

Notice whether the person has a pronounced or subtle philtrum (the groove between the base of the nose and upper lip).

Lips can be pouty, thick and full, thin, asymmetric, smooth, narrow, round, wide, fallen (the corner of the lips are tilted downwards) or 'oomph' (a defined and shaped upper lip, with a heart-shaped outline).

Teeth can vary from a celebrity set of pearly whites to protruding 'buck teeth', chipped, uneven or decayed. Individuals may also have dental devices like braces or replacement gold teeth.

Ears

The shape of your ears is unique. In fact, there is research into using ear shapes as an alternative biometric to iris or fingerprint scans.[22] Ears can have free, attached or partially attached earlobes. They may be large or small, flat or protruding, and varying in the amount of convolution.

Skin

Skin tone varies significantly according to tanning or race. It can be smooth or wrinkled. There can be blemishes such as moles, pimples, liver spots or acne. A person may have piercings or tattoos.

In general, people find it harder to discriminate between faces of races other than their own. This leads them to think that there are fewer differences between faces in particular ethnic groups. It is not racism, just a psychological phenomenon.

Research by Daniel Levin, PhD, a cognitive psychologist at Kent State University,[23] suggests that 'people place inordinate emphasis on race categories – whether someone is white, black or Asian – ignoring information that would help them recognize people as individuals'. Levin explains, 'When a white person looks at another white person's nose, they're likely to think to themselves, "That's John's nose." When they look at a black person's nose, they're likely to think, "That's a black nose."' It is possible to train yourself to recognize cross-race faces. 'If you really had to reorganize your whole face recognition system and build up a lifetime's worth of experience in order to recognize cross-race faces effectively, you'd think it would take a long time,' Levin argues. 'But it really doesn't seem to.'

Using business cards

Business cards are very useful as an *aide-memoire* after meeting someone.

You have the opportunity to look at the written name and the face at the same time, thereby making a visual link in your memory. I try to make life easier for people by having my photograph printed on my card.

In Asian cultures the presentation of a business card is very ritualized and ceremonial. The etiquette is to present it with both hands, maybe with a slight bow. It is believed that the card is an extension of the person and must be treated with respect, closely observed, and kept safely, though never placed in a back trouser pocket that you will sit on.

This is the height of disrespect. Never make notes on a card in Asian cultures as it is seen as akin to writing on the person's face.

Remembering surnames

In the Middle Ages names were related to professions, like Mr Farmer, or to geographical features, such as Mr Hill, and were practical ways of identifying the people in your village. Sometimes surnames were derived from the father's first name, like Johnson (the son of John), or from appearance, such as Mr White, or disposition (Mr Moody). Between the eleventh and sixteenth centuries, surnames became formalized and passed down from father to son.

Of course, nowadays a person's name has no relationship with his or her appearance or profession. You never meet 'Mr Web-Designer' or 'Miss Accountant'. However, if you know the origin and meaning of a name, you can use this to help remember it. For example, a cooper makes barrels, so if you meet Mrs Cooper you can imagine her wearing a barrel round her neck like a Saint Bernard rescue dog. We will talk more about facial associations with names later.

Here are some common surnames and their meanings.

Professions

Alderman – title initially given to a village headman or elder (man), and later, in the Middle Ages, to the governor of a guild

Archer / Bowman – a professional soldier skilled at firing arrows

Baker – a baker

Barber – the barber of the Middle Ages not only cut hair and shaved beards, but also acted as a surgeon and tooth-puller

Bishop – the early Christians adopted the word for the headman of their local communities, and from the fourth century AD it was applied to a religious leader

Brewer – a brewer of beer or ale

Brooke – Norman French 'broc', meaning a 'pitcher' or 'ewer'. Someone who delivered fresh water from such a vessel

Butcher – a supplier of meat

Carpenter – someone who works with wood

Chambers / Chamberlain – an officer charged with the management of his lord's private living quarters

Chandler – a maker or seller of candles

Cheeseman – a maker or seller of cheese

Clarke / Clark – any literate man, particularly a priest of minor orders, a secretary or scholar

Collier – a coal miner or burner of charcoal

Cook – a cook or seller of cooked meats

Cooper – a barrel maker

Driver – a driver of horse or oxen teams

Farmer – a farmer

Farrier – a person who shoes horses

Ferry – someone who operates a ferry, or who lives by a ferry

Fisher – a fisherman

Foreman – the manager of a large farm or estate

Forrester – an officer in charge of the King's forest

Gardner – head gardener of a noble or even royal house

Groom – a man-servant

Hunter – a hunter of game such as stags and wild boars, a pursuit restricted to the ranks of the nobility in the Middle Ages, but also a nickname for both bird catchers and poachers

Knight – most likely a servant in a knight's household

Mason – a skilled stonemason, one who had served his time as an apprentice to a master craftsman

Miller – someone in charge of a mill where corn was ground into flour

Nunn – probably originally either an occupational name for a male who worked at a nunnery, or for an actor who played the part of a nun in a travelling theatre

Patel – Indian origin, originally meaning 'headman' or 'village chief'. The record keeper named by princely rulers in Gujarat to keep track of the crops, 'pat' being a parcel of land

Plumber / Plumer – a worker in lead

Porter – the gatekeeper of a town, or a doorkeeper

of a large house, or a man who carries loads for a living

Rider – a messenger on horseback

Shepherd – someone who tends sheep

Shoemaker / Schumacher (German) – a cobbler or maker of shoes

Skinner – someone who prepared hides or pelts of animals. A member of the Worshipful Company of Skinners

Smith / Goldsmith – a blacksmith – worker in iron / gold

Tanner – a leather maker from animal skins and hides

Taylor / Tailor – a clothes maker

Thatcher – someone employed to repair or construct thatched roofs

Tyler – a maker or layer of tiles

Waterman – a boatman or a water-carrier

Weaver – a maker of cloth

Wright – a maker of machinery or objects, mostly in wood

Wainwright / Cartwright – a 'wain' is a cart (as in John Constable's painting *The Hay Wain*) so wainwrights and cartwrights build carts

Wheelwright – a maker of wheels

Zimmerman – Germanic occupational surname for a carpenter

Geographical or topographical links

In medieval times a visit to the next village was a major journey, and a visit to a city was something very special indeed. Hence the surnames 'York', 'London' or 'Lincoln' for people who have visited these places and returned.

If a name ends in 'ton', it is most likely from 'tun' meaning village. 'Alderton' means 'the village by the alder wood'. Many other names derive from woodland: Forest, Wood, Oakley, Birch, Beech, Underwood, Smallwood, etc.

Attwater describes somebody who lived by water. Names such as 'Ford' and 'Marsh' have similar associations with streams or rivers. The name 'Wells' derives from the pre-seventh-century word 'waella', which describes not a well but a spring. 'Mead' means a water meadow.

More obvious topographical names include 'Hill', 'Dale', 'Downs', 'Fields' (meaning open pasture) and similarly 'Fielding' or 'Greenfield'. 'Church' relates to someone living near to the village church.

Like father, like son

Any name that ends in 'son' originates from a father's name. Adamson (son of 'Adam'), Bryson (son of 'Brice'. Brice is a form of the Welsh name 'Rhys', meaning rashness), Carlson, Davidson, Ericson, Frederickson, Gregson, Higson, Jackson, Johnson, Morrison, Peterson, Robertson, Stevenson, Watson, etc.

The common Welsh name 'Jones' is a form of the name John, ultimately from the Hebrew 'Yochanan' meaning 'Jehovah has favoured me (with a son)'.

In Scotland the prefix 'Mac', or its shortened form 'Mc', denotes 'son of'. For example, 'MacPherson' comes from the

Gaelic 'Mac an Phearsain' meaning 'son of the parson' or 'MacDonald' (son of Donald). Similarly, MacKenzie means 'the son of Coinneach', from 'cainnechus' meaning fair skinned.

Other name origins

The name 'Ball' has a number of possible derivations. It may originate from a nickname for someone who was either bald or short and rotund. Alternatively it may relate to a person who lived on a knoll or a rounded hill. A third possibility is that it originates from the old Norse word 'bal' meaning torture or pain.

The surnames 'Badger', 'Wolf' and 'Fox' are named after the animals. 'Raven' and 'Crow' probably relate to someone with dark hair. Other names derived from birds include Lark, Hawk, Swan, Nightingale and Finch.

There are a number of names relating to colours. 'Blue' – someone with blue eyes; 'Brown' – from complexion, hair colour or clothes; 'Gray' / 'Grey' – a man with grey hair or beard; 'Green' – maybe someone who lives near the village green or played the part of the 'Green Man' in springtime or May Day celebrations; 'Black' – possibly a nickname given by the invading Angles and Saxons to the native Celts and Britons who were darker haired and darker skinned than themselves; conversely 'White' may have been an ethnic term given to Vikings or Anglo-Saxons, who were pale in hair and complexion compared with the Celts; 'Pink' – a nickname given to a bright, chirpy person, thought to be as active and cheerful as a chaffinch.

Remembering first names

First names come in an even greater variety than surnames. As they are usually not passed down through generations, they are more prone to changes due to social attitudes, celebrity influences and fashion.

There are a number of different lists of popular baby names published each year. According to the website 'Bounty Baby Club',[24] the top five baby names for girls and boys born in the first half of 2016 were as follows:

Girls:
1. Isla
2. Amelia
3. Ava
4. Freya
5. Evie

Boys (all unchanged since 2013):
1. Alfie
2. Oscar
3. Teddy
4. Harry
5. Jack

Where do first names come from?

First names come from a variety of sources. Focusing on the origins of names might give you imagery to make the first names more memorable.

1. Botany
Hyacinth, Cherry, Violet, Lily, Rose, Daisy, Iris,

Poppy, Ivy, Willow, Holly, Myrtle, Rowan, Olive
(Oliver / Olivia), Fleur (French for flower) and
Laura (from laurel)

2. *Gods or religious figures*
Mohammed – from the prophet
Angela – from angel
Roman goddesses – Diana, Flora and Luna
— *Biblical (Hebrew) names:*
Gabrielle – God is mighty
Jacob (James) – follower
Noah – rest
John (Jack) – Jehovah has been gracious
Peter – rock
Thomas – twin
Simon – He has heard
Matthew – gift of Jehovah
Nathanael – gift of God
Christian – belonging to Christ

3. *Characteristics or disposition*
Agatha – good
Alan – harmony
Alexander – defender of men
Amanda – loveable
Amelia – struggling, labour
Amy – beloved
Andrew – manly
Ann (Hannah) – grace
Arnold – eagle strength
Bridget – strength
Celeste – heavenly

Charles (Charlie) – manly
Donald – world chief
Edward – rich guard
Emma – whole, universal
Fay – faith
Frieda – peace
Henry (Harry) – house ruler
Lionel – young lion
Nigel – champion
Sophie – wisdom
Timothy – honoured of God
Verity – truth
Zoe – life

4. Months or seasons
Avril / April, May, June, summer, autumn

5. Places
Isla (river in Scotland)
Luke (from 'Lucania', a region in southern Italy)

6. Roman/Latin names
Emily – female form of 'Emil', from the Roman
    family name Aemilius
Mark – probably derived from the god 'Mars'

Attitude and practice

Approach the business of memorizing names with a positive attitude. Be playful and treat it like a game. It takes
practice to be able to memorize names quickly and effec-

tively. You can use LinkedIn or Facebook to find a wide range of unusual names with profile pictures. This lets you try strategies in a safe environment. It doesn't matter if you forget the name of a complete stranger you may never meet in real life.

Set yourself manageable goals to improve step by step. If you would normally expect to remember the names of five people at a networking event or party with forty people present, try next time to memorize six. This means you are not under stress to memorize everyone. You will probably exceed your goal. This gives you positive reinforcement. If you have a disaster and call someone by the wrong name or have a lapse of memory, this is absolutely fine. Analyse why you made the mistake and try to avoid doing the same thing again in the future.

Tackling unusual names

If you are confronted with an unusual name, you need to break it down into manageable components and form an image for each. In memory championships, competitors are given photographs of faces with complicated names to memorize. Here are a few examples of names from the 2015 UK Open:

> Sorasit Borg – On a seesaw a sitting Borg drone from *Star Trek* (or if you prefer, Tennis player Björn Borg).

> Frode Janowicz – Frodo Baggins (from *The Lord of the Rings*) and a janitor are shopping in Wickes DIY store.

Hyunsun Lite – Hyundai car shining in the sunlight.

Zhu Jayawardene – With a trophy in the form of a shoe (Zhu), American TV host Jay Leno awards Dean Martin.

In the competition you need to get the correct spelling but of course in real life, pronunciation is more important.

The location mnemonic technique

We talked about the importance of location to memory in Chapter Four. You can apply imagined locations to help you memorize names.

Look carefully at the person and think if they remind you of someone. Does he or she look like anyone you know? Do they resemble a celebrity or a famous politician? When I was at university there was a professor who bore an uncanny resemblance to John Cleese and I have a friend who looked like Russian leader Vladimir Lenin. Alternatively, do they remind you of a stereotypical accountant, lawyer, doctor, computer geek or other profession?

Let the resemblance trigger a location in your mind. If you think the person looks like a bank manager, imagine the local branch of your bank. If they look like a politician, imagine Westminster. You can now use the location as a context for the name.

For example, you meet someone with name is 'Lionel Hill' and he looks a little like Barack Obama. My location is the White House lawn in Washington D.C. where I position images associated to the name. You may remember from earlier in this chapter that 'Lionel' means a young lion and 'Hill' is obviously a hill. I imagine a huge hill has suddenly sprouted in front of the White House and stranding proudly atop it is a lion cub (picture Simba from *The Lion King*). Next time you meet Mr Hill his face will once again trigger a recollection of Barack Obama and stimulate the sequence of associations leading to his name.

The facial features mnemonic technique

If the person doesn't remind you of anyone, you can use attributes of the face as the basis of your associations. Notice any outstanding features as discussed earlier. Does the individual have a prominent nose or deeply coloured eyes, etc.?

Picture the face in your mind, taking particular notice of the salient characteristics you identified. Imagine him or her like a cartoonist's caricature. If you can make a direct link with the name, i.e. someone called Iris with large eyes, then that will be enough to trigger your memory.

If nothing obvious springs to mind, modify the image in your imagination to match the name. For example, you meet some called Poppy McDonald. She has a wide mouth and small ears. You can imagine her face with bright red poppies springing from her ears and a whole McDonald's hamburger gripped between her teeth.

Note: it is generally a good policy to never reveal exactly how you remember someone's name! Even if you have positive associations, he or she is almost certain to be offended.

Exercise: five-minute names and faces

You will see opposite a series of ten faces with their names written underneath. Try to apply the techniques discussed in this chapter to associate the names with the faces. Give yourself five minutes' memorization time. On the following page you will be given the same faces in a different order and you need to write the correct names beneath each.

This is the same format as at national memory championships, with the exception that you have ten faces whereas competitors are given fifty-eight in five minutes. The current world record for the five-minute event is ninety-seven points (forty-eight faces) by Katie Kermode from England.

Check your answers and give yourself one point per correct name (i.e. two points per correctly identified face).

Toby Townrow

Pitima Tongme

Andy Fong

David Hyner

Julie Orton

Chris Day

Svetlana Nadtoka

Lex McKee

Elaine Colliar

Mikiko Chikada

Summary

- Memorizing names is the number one memory problem.

- When being introduced to someone:

  - Be focused, attentive and listen carefully to the name.

  - If in doubt, confirm that you heard it correctly.

  - Try to take control of the pace of introductions. Exchange a few words.

  - For the time you're with them, show a genuine interest in the person.

  - Closely observe the features of the face.

- Study the origins of names.

- Practise! You can find lots of names and faces on Facebook or LinkedIn.

- Improve step by step and set yourself manageable goals.

- If you make mistakes, analyse and learn from them.

- Tackle unusual names by breaking them down into chunks and thinking up associated images for each part.

- Try location and feature mnemonic techniques.

7:

HOW TO MEMORIZE PASSWORDS AND FORMULAE

Secure Internet passwords and mathematical formulae are two of the most complex types of information that you are ever likely to need to memorize. This may seem daunting, but you already have most of the techniques in place. A little more work is needed to learn some additional associations, but the process is much simpler than you think.

Cyber security

According to *Newsweek*,[25] 'Of the people on the internet in 2016, there are those who have been breached by hackers and those who just don't know it yet. It's terrifying to realize your sense of security is more like an illusion than a guarantee.' In a world of online banking and e-commerce where sensitive data is stored online, it is vital to take precautions to safeguard your data with strong passwords. Some general safeguards are:

1. Avoid dictionary words – hackers can easily test thousands of word combinations.

2. Don't use birth dates or other personal information that can be guessed or discovered from your online profile.

3. Avoid obvious patterns like 'QWERTY', '12345', 'ABCDE' or repeated characters such as '111SS'.

4. Use a different password for each site. If one is compromised, then others will still be safe.

5. Don't reuse an old password.

6. The longer the password, the safer it is likely to be. Ten characters is a good safe length.

7. Mix lower and upper case letters with symbols.

8. Don't set your browser to remember passwords. It can be hacked, thus compromising everything it stores.

9. Don't send passwords in an email. List them in an unencrypted file or write them down near to your computer or digital device.

10. If you use a public computer, make sure you securely log out of any important sites. If possible, shut down and restart the computer when you've finished.

11. Make sure you install the latest security updates to your operating system or browser and keep your antivirus software up to date.

12. Don't open attachments to emails sent from an address you don't recognize. If an email appears to come from a friend and it doesn't feel like the way they write, check with them that it's genuine. Their account may have been compromised.

Unfortunately the harder a password is to hack, the harder it is to memorize. But what you have learned so far takes you a good way towards being able to memorize and recall long, complex and, above all, safe passwords.

The key to memorizing random information is to encode it into something intelligible that can then be symbolized, imagined and associated either with already known information or in a series of links.

Passwords need numbers, letters and symbols, each of which can be represented by an image or object.

Numbers and letters

You are already familiar with the Major System to convert two-digit numbers into objects. Single digits can be dealt with using the Number Shape or Number Rhyme Systems.

Letters of the alphabet can be converted into images of your choice in three different ways, as shown below. Take care that the images you choose do not match any of your Major System associations as this can lead to mistranslation when recalling.

Method 1

You can simply come up with twenty-six words that start with each letter of the alphabet in turn, for instance: Apple, Bear, Coat, Dog, Egg, Foot, Goat, Hat, Ice, Jet, Key, Lamp, etc.

Method 2

Alternatively, you can use a rhyme or homophone to associate the letter with an object. I have given my list opposite but you are encouraged for come up with your own associations, as you were with the Major System digits 00–99.

A – hay

B – bee

C – sea

D – deer

E – ear

F – fir (tree or cone)

G – jeans

H – H-bomb (mushroom cloud)

I – eye

J – jay (bird)

K – cake

L – shell

M – Emma (someone you know called Emma or a famous Emma such as actress Emma Thompson)

N – hen

O – oak

P – pea

Q – (snooker) cue

R – arm

S – snake (hisses and same shape)

T – tea (or teapot)

U – U-boat

V – Winston Churchill making the 'V' for victory sign

W – two sheep (double ewe)

X – X-ray

Y – Y-fronts

Z – zebra

Method 3

If you are familiar with the NATO phonetic alphabet, this can provide twenty-six associated images:

A   Alfa – an Alfa Romeo car

B   Bravo – an audience applauding

C   Charlie – someone you know called Charlie, or *Peanuts* comic strip character Charlie Brown

D   Delta – Delta airlines aeroplane

E   Echo – calling out and hearing an echo bounce back or the rock band Echo & the Bunnymen

F   Foxtrot – dancers, perhaps on *Strictly*

G   Golf – a golfer or a set of clubs

H   Hotel – a hotel, or a hotel manager such as Basil Fawlty

I   India – a plate of delicious curry

J   Juliet – someone you know called Juliet or the Shakespearian character

K   Kilo – a heavy weight

L   Lima – the Madagascan ring-tailed lemur (or, as Lima is the capital of Peru, you could imagine someone playing Peruvian panpipes)

M   Mike – someone you know called Mike or a microphone

N   November – fireworks (from Guy Fawkes Night)

O   Oscar – an actor with the award

P   Papa – your father

Q   Quebec – someone waving the Canadian flag

R Romeo – someone you know called Romeo, e.g. Romeo Beckham, or the Shakespearian character

S Sierra – a Ford car of the same name

T Tango – orange fizzy drink

U Uniform – anyone in uniform such as a nurse or police officer

V Victor – someone you know called Victor or the character Victor Meldrew from the BBC sitcom *One Foot in the Grave*

W Whiskey – a bottle or glass of Scotch whisky

X X-ray – an X-ray photograph

Y Yankee – someone waving the American flag or a baseball player from the New York Yankees

Z Zulu - a Zulu warrior brandishing a spear

You can denote upper or lower-case letters by modifying the images in a way similar to that of masculine or feminine words in Chapter Three. The images for capital letters could be huge and lower-case letters tiny. You could encase upper-case letters in ice or colour them differently. Do whatever feels easiest for you, as long as there is a clear distinction.

Symbols

Come up with an object suggested by the symbol. See a selection below with my associations:

! Exclamation mark – a road sign warning danger ('!' in a red triangle)

@ At – a hat

Hash – a hash brown

£ Pound sterling – a pound coin

$ Dollar – an American dollar bill

% Per cent – a Euro one-cent coin

^ Caret or Circumflex – a carrot

& Ampersand – a hamper full of sand

* Asterisk or star – the comic character Asterix the Gaul or a starfish

/ slash – a urinal or, less vulgar, a silk sash, or musician 'Slash', lead guitarist of the American hard-rock band Guns N' Roses

– Minus or subtraction – Midas (mythical king whose touch turned objects to gold) or a subway train

+ Plus or Addition – a pair of plus-four trousers; someone you know called Adam or Biblical first man

? Question mark – a quizmaster (or specifically actor Mark Williams who presents BBC daytime game show *The Link*, better known as Arthur Weasley in the *Harry Potter* films)

> Greater than – a cheese grater

< Less than – a teacher giving a lesson

= Equals – an Eagle

Creating a journey of numbers, letters and symbols

Putting this all together, you take each symbol, letter, single number or pair of numbers in the password in turn, convert them into objects using the schemes above and place them at locations along a mental journey. Add an extra location at the start to symbolize the website that the password applies to. For example, a jungle for Amazon, a photo album for Facebook, Sherlock Holmes with his magnifying glass for a search engine, etc.

If you have the ten-digit password *34^fG*21&J* and it is your Facebook login password, you need a nine-location journey populated as follows:

Location one: Facebook – a photo album

Location two: 34 – mare (major system)

Location three: ^ – carrot

Location four: f – a tiny (because lower case) bonsai fir tree

Location five: G – a large (because upper case) pair of jeans

Location six: * – a starfish

Location seven:– 21 – net (Major System)

Location eight: & – a hamper full of sand

Location nine: J – a large colourful jay

Once you have reviewed the nine-location journey a few times you will easily be able to recall the password. This is very secure. I can't say it could never be hacked but it would take a long time to do so. Even so, it is good practice to change your password from time to time.

An alternative method

Complexity, and hence security, is a trade-off against the amount of work involved. Creating a journey of up to eleven locations per password for each site may seem like a lot of work.

Some of the sites you use probably have few consequences if you have a unique password and it is compromised. I have accounts on Hightail for sending large files and Bitly for shortening long URLs. Neither of these have any financial information so the worst anyone could do is see what links I have previously shared or send a file purporting to be from me.

If you can live with good but not exceptional security, you can go down a simpler route. Think back to Chapter 1 and linguistic memory systems. It is possible to create acronyms that are easy to remember and use them as passwords. You need to be a bit creative to involve numbers and symbols but it is simpler than using a journey.

Taking the following quote from Macbeth's soliloquy, Act 2, Scene 1, 'Is this a dagger which I see before me . . .' could give 'ITADWICB4me'. Note that the acronym doesn't give any clues to upper or lower case. As I mentioned in Chapter One, acronyms are open to paraphrasing. If you missed out the word 'which', and hence 'w', it would still make sense but would obviously be rejected when entered as the password.

You can incorporate symbols to a certain extent. For example, 'I love New York State' gives rise to 'I<3NYSt8:-)'. The 'less than' symbol followed by a '3' for a heart and the ':-)' a smiley.

Mathematical formulae

A side benefit of learning associations for the alphabet and for symbols is that you can use basically the same system for memorizing mathematical equations and formulae. You need to create a few more associations for specific mathematical terms and some Greek letters (e.g. 'alpha', 'beta', 'pi' or 'theta').

For example, Newton's formula for gravitation is:

$$F = G\frac{mM}{r^2}$$

where:

F = gravitational force between the objects
G = the gravitational constant
m = mass of the first object
M = mass of the second object
r = the distance separating the objects

In addition to the alphabetic associations already discussed we need 'squared', for which I think of a 'squid'. When reading the formula you would use the word 'over', rather than slash, for the division part so I associate a 'cricket ball' (as 'overs' is a cricketing term).

To memorize the formula you need a six-location journey populated as follows:

Location one: F – a fir tree

Location two: = – an eagle

Location three: G – a pair of jeans

Location four: mM – you could have big Emma with her small counterpart in a single location

Location five: over – a cricket ball

Location six: r² – an arm being gripped by the
   tentacles of a squid

For a much more detailed discussion of the method see
How to Remember Equations and Formulae by Phil Chambers
and James Smith.

Exercise

Memorize the following using the techniques discussed in
this chapter:

1. The password 89£H*k+%72

2. The formula for compound interest:

$$A = P\left(1 + \frac{r}{n}\right)^{nt}$$

where:

A = amount

P = principle amount (initial investment)

r = annual interest rate (as a decimal)

n = number of times the interest is compounded
   per year

t = number of years

Hint: this breaks down as:

Location one: 'A'

Location two: '='

Location three: 'P'

Location four: '(' (open bracket; an unbuttoned open jacket)

Location five: '1' (number shape or rhyme)

Location six: '+'

Location seven: 'r'

Location eight: over

Location nine: 'n'

Location ten: ')' (close bracket; a buttoned-up closed jacket)

Location eleven: to the power (I use a battery)

Location twelve: 'nt' (place two images at location)

Summary

- The characters of the password need to be represented by objects, which are positioned along a mental journey.

- Numbers:
  - Pairs of numbers use the Major System codes.
  - Single numbers use Number Shape or Rhyme Systems.

- Letters can be converted to objects by:
  - Choosing a word for each letter based on its initial.
  - Making associations based on the NATO phonetic alphabet.

- Using a word that is a rhyme or homophone of the letter.

- Symbols are converted to objects by creating an association with the name of the symbol.

- Upper and lower-case letters are represented by modifying the object's size or some other characteristic.

- An alternative method is to make up acronyms for passwords. Make sure you still include symbols, numbers, capital and lower-case letters.

- You can memorize mathematical formulae in the same way as a password by converting each term into an object and placing it along a mental journey in sequence.

- Some additional mathematical symbols and Greek letters need to be encoded into objects.

8:

MIND MAPPING SKILLS

It is unfortunately a fantasy that we only have to pass tests in school and that we can put them behind us in adulthood. Everyone needs to be a lifelong learner. The pace of change is such that if we don't continually study, we will be left behind.

Very few people will have the same job forever. Many retrain for a new career path or to achieve promotion. Professional exams are becoming ever more important for lawyers, financial advisors, doctors, accountants and those in other fields. In this chapter, I will explain how memory plays a vital role in study and how you can optimize your learning.

One of the most common criticisms made against mnemonics by educationalists is that they do not aid understanding, that they promote a blind, unthinking, parrot-fashion regurgitation of dissociated data. True, you don't need to understand something in order to memorize it. But consider the opposite scenario – what use is it to understand without the help of memory? If you understand something and then promptly forget it, you don't gain or accumulate knowledge. Learning and study require under-standing *and* retention in order to be in any way effective. Both aspects reinforce each other.

The technique of Mind Mapping that we will consider in this chapter is an effective combination of a mnemonic and a thinking tool, thereby satisfying both memory and understanding.

What is Mind Mapping?

Mind Mapping is described as a 'graphical thought organization technique' and was developed by Tony Buzan in the late 1960s.

Necessity is often the mother of invention and so it was with Mind Mapping. While at university, Tony Buzan found himself struggling with his studies. The harder he worked and the more notes he took, the worse his grades were becoming. There were three options. Firstly, do less work and inevitably fail. Secondly, redouble his efforts and take more notes – a method that clearly wasn't working. Third, find a better way to take notes. Tony took this option. After a great deal of research and self-experimentation, Mind Mapping began to take shape.

Tony Buzan says, 'In the early stages of developing the Mind Map, I envisaged Mind Mapping being used primarily for memory. However, after months of discussion, my brother Barry convinced me that creative thinking was an equally important application of this technique.'[26]

Barry Buzan explains:

> What attracted me about Mind Mapping was not the note-taking application that had captivated Tony, but the note-making one. I needed not only to organise a growing mass of research data, but also to clarify my thoughts on my thesis of the convoluted political question of why peace movements almost always fail to

achieve their stated objectives. My experience was that Mind Maps were a more powerful tool for thinking because they enabled me to sketch out the main ideas and to see quickly and clearly how they related to each other. They provided me with an exceptionally useful intermediate stage between the thinking process and actually committing words to paper. I soon realised that the problem of bridging the gap between thinking and writing was a major deciding factor in success or failure for my fellow postgraduate students. Many failed to bridge this gap. They became more and more knowledgeable about their research subject but less and less able to pull all the details together in order to write about it.

As I write this book, I am using Mind Mapping software to organize my ideas in exactly the way Barry Buzan explains. It enables me to think about what I write before I put it into sentences and paragraphs. As a result, I need to spend less time redrafting as I know what I want to say from the outset.

How to Mind Map

The process of creating a Mind Map follows a series of prescribed laws or rules. These are as follows:

1. Gather your materials

Mind Maps aim to summarize everything on a single page. This enables you to clearly see associations and connections. To facilitate the expansive development of ideas it is best practice to use a large sheet of paper, typically A3 in size. Use good-quality plain paper without lines or squares that would otherwise constrain the flow of thoughts to a linear pattern. Buy an artist's sketchpad or raid the photocopier paper tray. If using Mind-Mapping software, you have a virtually infinite canvas to work on that you can zoom into or scroll through.

For study purposes, I think that hand-drawn Mind Maps are preferable. You have the kinaesthetic feedback from the paper and pens, and the act of thinking about how to draw an image helps commit it to memory. Software tends to be better for presentations and business applications. However, it is a matter of personal preference – use whatever you feel more comfortable with.

Mind Maps make use of colour (see below) so you will also need a set of coloured pens. These need to be sufficiently fine tipped to enable you to clearly write with them as well as draw lines. Try to have at least four colours but preferably ten or more. I routinely carry a set of Stabilo Point 88 pens with twenty-five colours in a convenient fabric case that rolls up compactly. Staedtler Triplus Fineliners are also excellent and come in twenty colours.

If you don't have the best materials to hand, this doesn't preclude Mind Mapping. I've seen Mind Maps made on the back of an envelope, paper napkins, beer mats and even scratched on a beach with a stick.

2. Choose a vivid central image

Orientate your paper to landscape view (long edge across the top and bottom). If your branches spread more horizontally than vertically, they will be easier to read. Start in the centre of your paper with an image that represents the topic being considered. Make this as visually stimulating as possible. It can be multi-coloured or patterned and employ three-dimensional perspective to make it stand out. An aesthetically pleasing image keeps your focus and stimulates thoughts more effectively than a monochrome word.

Many Mind Map beginners are tempted to surround their image with a circle, oval or rectangular box. This enclosure acts like a fence to barricade and restrict the development of ideas from the centre. It is preferable to allow the outline of the image to make its own unique shape. If desired, you can supplement, but not substitute, the image with a word.

Don't worry if you feel your drawing skills let you down. In most cases a Mind Map is for your own personal thinking process and so doesn't have to be an artistic masterpiece. As long as you can recognize what you were trying to represent that is fine. If you struggle to draw from memory, find an image to copy. If you're using Mind-Mapping software, you can import Clipart, use built-in central images or make use of Google Images. Sourcing images from the internet is fine for your own personal purposes, but if you intend to sell or distribute your Mind Maps, make sure you're not infringing copyright.

3. Create curvilinear branches

Branches on Mind Maps are bold, curved, tapering lines that connect to the central image like branches emanating from the trunk of a mature tree. Each branch contains a 'Basic Ordering Idea' written above it. If the Mind Map is representing a book, these could be the chapter headings.

The aim is to group related information together, thus making it more intelligible.

Thinner, curved sub-branches are connected to the end of the main branches with additional ideas. Likewise, third and fourth levels of information are added, with lines always being connected to the endpoints of previous lines and radiating outwards.

Make sure that the length of the line matches the length of the word (or image) placed on it. When Mind Mapping by hand it is clearer and quicker to use single pen strokes for second-level branches onwards. When using Mind-Mapping software line weight is automatically decreased as you move out.

There are multiple reasons why curved lines are used in preference to straight or angular lines. These include:

- *Aesthetics* – Curved lines are more appealing to the eye than straight lines. A Mind Map replicates forms found in nature from neurons in the brain to river deltas viewed from space.

- *Better use of the page* – Curves enable far better use of space. As the Mind Map grows, curves naturally flow into free space. Straight lines become crowded and run a greater risk of colliding with each other, thereby closing off the development of ideas.

- *Visual variety* – Curved lines allow each Mind Map to have a unique structure. Straight or angular branches give rise to uniformity and monotony. This causes different Mind Maps to interfere with each other when you attempt to memorize them, resulting in poor recall and ultimately confusion. Images and colours play a similar role.

4. Add key words

Place key words above branches so that the word follows the curve of the line. To aid clarity and readability, words are printed rather than using 'joined-up' handwriting. You may use capitals or lower-case lettering. Generally use bigger and bolder writing near the centre, getting smaller and lighter as you work outwards. If you are using software, you can choose various fonts to achieve this.

You should always use single words and avoid sentences or phrases. The use of sentences has two very important negative consequences. Firstly, a sentence requires a very long line. This reduces the scope for sub-branches to be added. It breaks up the network of associations and restricts idea generation. Secondly, and potentially even more damaging, sentences imprison thought.

Imagine you were creating a Mind Map reviewing performance. You create a branch that reads 'Unsuccessful Product Launch'. This is a statement of fact. There is nowhere to branch off from this.

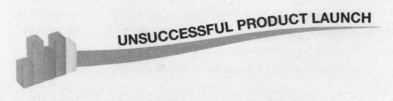

If you can break the statement down into keywords, you can create multiple endpoints from which to develop. You can think about factual aspects of the launch, things that were successful, things that were unsuccessful and the reasons why. This gives a much fuller analysis, indicates lessons to be learned and provides a more realistic picture.

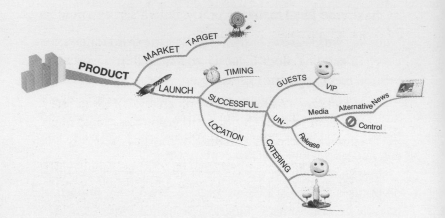

The notion that single words are sufficient to represent complex information is often challenging to novice Mind Mappers. They are afraid that the words will lead to ambiguity and they won't remember what they mean. The key thing to appreciate is that the Mind Map was never designed to be an unambiguous communication tool. The words act as triggers for the person who created the Mind Map to recollect what they were thinking when they chose those words. Of course, your associations and choice of words will be unique to you. The question of whether you'll forget what the words mean relies on whether you review the Mind Map or not. I will cover review in detail in Chapter Nine. Trust in yourself and use single words.

5. Play with colour

Each branch is given its own colour. It is usually best to use contrasting colours. For example, a blue branch next to a red one will be more distinct than an orange one.

Everyone loves colour but its use on a Mind Map is not

to make your Mind Map look pretty. Colour serves a number of practical purposes, as follows:

- *Clarity* – Colour helps us to discern differences and therefore extract meaning.

- *Chunking* – As each main branch and its 'twigs' are the same colour this helps to group associated ideas into chunks of information.

- *Colour coding* – Colours can be used to encode extra information without the need for additional words that could potentially clutter a complex Mind Map. In a meeting context you could make all action points red or assign each person a colour to track their contribution.

- *Creativity* – Colour increases engagement and attention and promotes creativity.

- *Highlighting important points* – Using a different colour from that which predominates on a branch is an efficient way of drawing attention to salient points.

6. Add more images

In addition to the central image, use images throughout your Mind Map. Place them on lines in the same way you've added key words – don't leave images floating in empty space. They need to be part of the network of associations that the Mind Map forms.

As with colour, images are not just used for decoration but play a vital role in thinking. Images are more memorable than words. A picture often stimulates thoughts better than a word, thereby boosting creativity. Liberal use of pictures enlivens the Mind Map, making it unique and much more engaging.

Some images have specialist roles. Symbols are used as a shorthand for words. For example, it is quicker and more compact to use a letter 'i' in a circle than to write the word 'information'. A red 'L' in a square, as used for learner drivers, can represent 'learning' and a quick sketch of an elephant can symbolize 'memory'. You can develop your own vocabulary of commonly used symbols.

Codes employ similar icons but for a different purpose. These can show linkages between related ideas at different places on your Mind Map. If the same idea crops up several times, you can place an icon, such as a star, next to each occurrence to identify the recurrent theme. You may also use arrows to show connections but these are best used sparingly as they can get complicated and tangled.

7. Build a structure

When creating your Mind Map, you don't need to sequentially complete a main branch and all its descendants before moving on to the next. You jump from branch to branch, adding information where it best fits as your ideas flow. The Mind Map is thus built up holistically. Despite the semi-random generation process, the end result is that information is organized in multiple ways:

- *Thematically* – The Mind Map is formed from Basic Ordering Ideas.

- *Hierarchically* – General ideas are near the centre, and more specific and detailed data is on the periphery.

- *Sequentially* – Imagine a clock face and the angle that the hour hand makes at two o'clock. This is typically our starting point on a Mind Map. We 'read' travelling outwards and clockwise. If an alternative sequence is intended, branches may be numbered.

- *Radiantly* – The Mind Map appears to unfurl like a flower.

What is more, a Mind Map lets you see context and inter-relationships between initially disparate ideas. This can lead to new insights which otherwise may not have come to light.

Why do Mind Maps help memory?

To evaluate a mnemonic technique it makes sense to compare it against the primary memory principles. Think back to Chapter Two and we can see how Mind Mapping measures up.

Imagination
The word 'imagination' derives from the Latin *'imaginari'*, meaning 'to form a mental picture'. Images are the essence of imagination and are widely made use of in Mind Maps. Colour also stimulates imagination.

Association
The structure of a Mind Map is based on association. This is further extended with the use of arrows, numbers, symbols and patterns.

Location
Spatial layout and location of information on the page are

very important in Mind Mapping. Tony Buzan says, 'Leaving the right amount of space around each item gives your Mind Map order and structure. Taken to its logical conclusion, the space between items can be as important as the items themselves.'

SEAHORSE principles

Senses

Mind Maps are, of course, primarily visual but if you create them by hand there is a tactile, or kinaesthetic, aspect to them. When reviewing or 'reading' the Mind Map back to yourself, there is an internal auditory sense. More importantly, you can use images or words that evoke all the senses. Tony Buzan says:

> Wherever possible, you should include in your Mind Maps words or images that refer to the senses of sight, hearing, smell, taste, touch and kinaesthesia (physical sensation). This technique has been used by many of the famous memorizers to remember vast amounts of information, as well as by great writers and poets to make their creative work interesting, entertaining and memorable.

Exaggeration

Mind Maps encourage you to vary the size and font of your lettering to accentuate important points. Highlighting and the use of perspective to imply three dimensions are all examples of exaggeration and create many instances of the Von Restorff Effect.

Action

You can evoke action in your Mind Map by choice of words and images. You can imply movement with cartoon 'whizz' lines and bold, flowing branches.

Humour

I like to be playful and include visual puns in my Mind Maps. It has become a tradition for me to create an animated Mind Map Christmas card representing the words to a seasonal song with lots of images. These make liberal use of homophones and literalism. You can see examples on YouTube. Search for 'Mind Map Christmas card'.

Order

Mind Maps are very ordered and structured. The network of branches and associations ensure that all the information is connected appropriately. Mind Maps have a visual rhythm to them, which is also a form of order.

Repetition

Tony Buzan says the following on the subject of repetition in the context of Mind Maps and memory:

> Repetition assists in recalling information. By 're-viewing' information, the synaptic connections in your brain involved in a particular storage process are being reactivated. This makes these connections stronger and easier to access. This need for repetition is met by Mind Maps in two ways:
> 1. When you create a Mind Map, the data already

processed remains in eyesight all the time, since Mind Maps consist of only one page. This means that your brain is constantly repeating these data.

2. Mind Maps are condensed and invite you to look at them. The main elements of memory include imagination, colour, shape, association, structure and Loci (specific locations). All of these memory enhancers are the essential components of a Mind Map. Linear notes, by contrast, are monochromatic and anti-mnemonic.

It is also essential to review your Mind Maps after you have created them, in order to maintain recall and transfer the information into long-term memory (see Chapter Nine).

Symbols

As already mentioned, symbols, icons and images are an integral part of Mind Mapping.

Enjoy

Using images, colour and imagination makes studying with Mind Maps much more enjoyable than taking dull, boring, linear notes.

As you can see, Mind Mapping obeys the fundamentals of a mnemonic device whilst also promoting understanding. It is truly a remarkably powerful tool.

How to revise with Mind Maps

Revision for exams is traditionally a hard slog of going through key textbooks and notes made in class. Most students end up writing more notes or creating cards with bullet points. It is then a case of reading these over and over again until something sticks. It is tedious, boring and, as the exams get nearer, very stressful.

Mind Maps alleviate the pressure as they allow you to condense two years' worth of work into about ten sheets of paper. These can be pinned on the wall to be quickly and frequently reviewed. I will cover more about this in the next chapter.

Here is an overview of the process of creating a revision Mind Map:

1. Choose a unique central image representing the facet of the subject you will be revising. If it's electromagnetism in physics, you could draw a lightning bolt and a horseshoe magnet.

2. Create a main branch for each key area.

3. Start adding sub-branches, noting down anything you remember about the subject. As the Mind Map stimulates the flow of thoughts you may surprise yourself with how much you actually know.

4. When you've exhausted your existing knowledge go to your reference material, whether that is textbooks or notes you made in class. Read a paragraph and then add a few summary words to the Mind Map expanding on your existing structure.

5. Add as many images and diagrams as you can on

your Mind Map. These will stimulate your memory and make reviewing easier.

6. Add links and connections with arrows and codes.

7. If you find a particular part difficult, just skip over it and come back at the end. When you have more context surrounding the hard part it is likely to make better sense.

8. If your Mind Map seems to be getting too detailed, you may need to redraw a simplified version. Remember the Mind Map is supposed to trigger the memory of the information in your head, not to unambiguously record everything. Mind Maps need to be clear and easy to read but not necessarily beautifully neat. Clear thinking and a little messy is better than beautiful with little thought.

Review your Mind Maps regularly and practise redrawing them from memory. Look back at the original and compare it with the redrawn version. This will bring to light any gaps that need to be focused on.

Mega Mind Maps

One of the key factors of Mind Mapping is that everything is on one page. A Mega Mind Map consolidates multiple Mind Maps for a course of study onto one big-picture overview.

This will work best with an A1-size flipchart sheet or, if you don't have this size to hand, you can tape four sheets of A3 together.

The central image is the overarching topic, for example Physics.

The Basic Ordering Ideas, on main branches, are the central images of each of your ten or so Mind Maps already created for the facets of the subject. For example – radio-activity, energy, waves, electromagnetic radiation, forces and mechanics, etc.

The sub-branches of the Mega Mind Map correspond to the Basic Ordering Ideas of the individual Mind Maps.

Third-level branches include some of the details. You are not attempting to transfer all the information onto your Mega Mind Map but to get a helicopter view of the subject as a whole. This allows you to see new connections. For example, forces, energy and waves are intimately related. A deep understanding of this type is the difference between achieving an 'A' or an 'A*' grade.

Curriculum content

When you first begin studying a subject, it is a good idea to get an idea of the syllabus. You need a map of the territory that you'll be exploring and a Mind Map provides this. A bit like the Mega Mind Map that you create towards the end of studying a subject, this is a big-picture overview. The benefits of starting from the syllabus are that you can see where you're going, put your learning in context, track progress made and ensure everything is covered.

How to use Mind Maps as essay plans

Start with a 'quick idea generation' Mind Map. To do this, choose a central idea image based on the question that is being asked and break this down into Basic Ordering Ideas.

Note your thoughts as they come to you, adding branches where they best fit. Allow yourself to freely associate. Don't censor your ideas at this stage. Add arrows and codes to show cross-references. Include colour and images.

Essays follow a specific structure such as introduction and statement, argument, evidence and conclusions.

Create a new Mind Map that edits the information and draws it into a more structured format. The Basic Ordering Ideas should be based on the structural conventions.

This will allow you to write a first draft of the essay based on the Mind Map. Don't worry about grammar or spelling. Allow your ideas to flow. Skip difficult bits.

Finally spell check, correct grammar and fill in any gaps. Add any additional supporting evidence, quotes and references as required.

Case studies

As we have discussed so far, Mind Maps and mnemonics are very well suited to study and revision. The following case studies give a good indication of what is possible when the principles of Mind Mapping, and memory in general, are fully applied. The individuals mentioned below are not exceptionally gifted. They are ordinary people who have achieved extraordinary results.

Ten GCSEs in three months – James Lee's story

I first met James Lee while I was at Durham University studying Physics and Chemistry. He was in the year above me studying Psychology. James and I both used Mind Maps but I didn't know at the time what an impact they had had on him at school. Tony Buzan recounts James's story: 'At the age of fifteen James missed six months of schooling because of illness and was advised to go back a year in view of the fact that his GCSE examinations loomed on the horizon. James persuaded his teachers to let him "go for it" and started to Mind Map everything in sight! In just three months he did a year's work, and in ten examinations scored seven As and three Bs.'

Straight 'A's at A-Level – Elaine Colliar's story

'Fourteen students from four South London schools approached us with a single burning ambition: "Show us how to get 'A's in our A-levels and we will do it" – and they did! Despite three having dyslexia and one having cerebral palsy, ALL passed their exams with flying colours – an amazing forty-two "A" grades between them. One of the students decided to study for A-level Spanish with only six months to go before the exams "Because learning was now so easy – I wanted a new challenge".[27] This was achieved by teaching the students how to Mind Map, giving them some simple memory strategies and showing them how to manage their revision to make the best use of time.'

From teenage single mum to occupational psychologist – Bridget Hanna's story

'I'm told I was a literary and creative child who read voraciously, but school seemed more difficult for me than this auspicious start might suggest. It was not a place I enjoyed. I was a late bloomer who needed help with language and English. My handwriting still totally embarrasses me. (I have a tendency to not finish words as my brain seems to go too fast for my hand to catch up.) School rules drove me mad and this, coupled with an early tendency to solitude, meant that I didn't do well.

'I had both my children in my late teens. Learning how to be a mum was great, but I didn't have the energy for anything else. One day I realized I might need money and to get this I would have to get a job. The jobs that I was qualified for didn't pay well and weren't enjoyable – I needed a career. If I was going to give up time with my precious girls, it had to be for something worthwhile. My early career capitalized on my language skills, which by now were well developed. Soon I got interested in training and here I really found a home. I was particularly interested in why we did things in training in particular ways, and I started looking round for techniques to help my research. One of these was Mind Mapping: I really enjoyed learning about how the mind worked. At the same time my youngest daughter was struggling with dyslexia and I was finding ways to help her, so I signed up to take a psychology course in Child Development. It turns out I hated child development but a love of psychology was born. Tony Buzan was the first psychologist I knew. I was intrigued and decided this was something I might be able to do, so I enrolled on a BSc Honours course with the Open University. As I was interested in training and work I then went on to take an MSc in Occupational Psychology.

'By now you are probably thinking, "What's all this got to do with Mind Mapping?" Well, pretty much everything. You see, Mind Mapping helped me to organize and manage all the information I was accumulating. I made Mind Maps of each chapter or lecture as I went through my modules. At the end I made Master Mind Maps of the whole course. These were invaluable in revision as they showed connections between subject areas and gave me a visual to remember. Of course, this wasn't the only technique. I also used memory techniques to help with the dates of studies, and mental journeys to remember the pathways through the evidence. From teenage single mum to occupational psychologist, Mind Mapping played a part in virtually every major learning activity I did. Mind Mapping helped me build my confidence in learning because it made learning manageable for me. I don't always use it (and never tell Tony I don't always use the colours) but it has always remained something I can rely on when I'm thinking generatively or when I want to understand complex interrelations.

'Recently I finished my doctorate, and as I was standing on the stage to receive my PhD I paused to think about some of the people, organizations and skills that helped me get here. Mind Mapping was definitely one of them.'

Combining Mind Maps and mental journeys

Tony Buzan sees Mind Mapping as a panacea that can be used in any situation. Whilst it is very versatile, there are certain situations where a Mind Map is not the best tool for the job.

If you need to memorize a list with no particular structure, then transferring it to a Mind Map still gives you a list. It may have some colour and images added but, personally, I would find it far easier to use a mental journey or a Link System.

Another situation in which Mind Maps perform badly is the verbatim (word for word) memorization of text. Mind-mapping software lets you add 'box branches'. These can contain direct quotes but they disrupt the structure of a Mind Map and go against the rules described previously. Once again, a mental journey works better as described in Chapter Four when considering memorizing a speech.

Thirdly, mathematical equations are better memorized, as described in Chapter Seven.

Despite these limitations you do not have to completely abandon Mind Mapping for lists, quotes or equations. You can combine techniques.

Imagine you are studying mathematics. You have a Mind Map all about quadratic equations. These are just equations that have a 'squared' term somewhere in them. You can have all the details about what a graph of this type of equation looks like and how to solve by 'factoring' or 'completing the square'. The step-by-step format for these methods could be expressed using flow charts within the Mind Map. The final method for solving quadratic equations is by substitution into the 'quadratic formula'. I would memorize the formula with a mental journey and draw a picture of the first location on the Mind Map. When you review the Mind Map you will come to this picture and it will trigger the recollection of the formula whilst keeping it in the context of quadratic equations.

The same idea of an image to trigger a journey can be used for lists or lengthy direct quotes.

Another way to combine Mind Maps with mental journeys is to take the central images from your Mind Maps and position them in real locations. This helps keep track of multiple Mind Maps. Say you're studying six subjects with ten Mind Maps each. Decide on a zone for each subject. Imagine Biology in the living room, Chemistry in the kitchen, French in the bathroom, Geography in the bedroom, History in the garage and English Literature in the garden. Starting with Biology in the living room: if you have a Mind Map on genetics with a central image of a pair of jeans, imagine a pair of faded denim jeans draped over the sofa. If your next Mind Map is on the human skeletal system with a central image of a skeleton, you can imagine a skeleton dancing on the coffee table. As you imagine your journey around the house, you will 'see' each of your Mind Map central images. These trigger the memory of the associated Mind Maps in your mind's eye.

How to use Mind Maps in everyday life

An alternative definition of the Mind Map is as the 'Swiss Army Knife for the Brain', meaning that it has very many uses.

If you are writing a report, you can approach it in much the same way as you would an essay. This will speed up the process and improve the structure, thereby making it much more readable. You can even include your Mind Map in the executive summary. Any form of planning, from a family holiday to making a presentation or a business plan, can be facilitated with a Mind Map. You can use Mind Maps for goal setting, self-analysis or keeping a diary. Meeting minutes can be recorded in Mind Map form, reducing the need to spend lots of time typing them up. Because you are not having to write sentences, you can capture more – faster. Mind Maps can be combined with thinking tools like a SWOT (Strengths, Weaknesses, Opportunities, Threats) analysis, or PEST (Political, Economic, Social, Technological) macro-environment analysis to solve business problems. They go way beyond study mnemonics.

Summary

- Effective study requires a combination of memory and understanding. Mind Mapping is a tool that can achieve this.

- Mind Mapping adheres to a set of rules as follows:

  - Use a large sheet of blank paper.

  - Create a visually stimulating image in the centre of the page.

  - Add tapering, curved branches radiating out from the centre with a word or image on each.

  - Add additional, thinner, curved branches connected to the end of previously drawn branches with related ideas.

  - Use single key words or images placed on lines.

- Words are printed.

- Each branch, along with its associated 'twigs', is assigned a different colour.

- Mind Maps use images throughout.

• Despite being built up holistically Mind Maps end up being highly structured.

• Mind Maps adhere to memory the principles of 'Imagination-Association-Location' and 'SEAHORSE'.

• Mega Mind Maps summarize multiple topical Mind Maps to give an overview of an entire subject or course of study.

• You can summarize the whole syllabus of a subject with a Mind Map at the start of a course to put your learning into a wider context.

• Mind Maps can be used as essay plans.

• You can combine Mind Maps and mental journeys.

• Mind Maps have many applications.

9:

HOW TO SUSTAIN MEMORIES

It doesn't matter how well you memorize something – if you don't review, you will eventually forget it. However, with the correct scheduling of reviews, memories can last a lifetime. In this chapter, I will explain the psychology of forgetting and show you how to manage the review process.

Do you believe time management is important? It is actually impossible. Time manages itself perfectly well and has done so for more than thirteen billion years. You cannot create or destroy time. Even taking into account Einstein's theory of relativity, if you travel close to the speed of light, you still experience the same amount of time, even though this will be different relative to a stationary observer. The best you can do is to manage yourself and your actions in the context of time. The good news is that, when done correctly, managing your actions can greatly boost the efficiency of your memory.

The theory of remembering

In Chapter Four I mentioned Hermann Ebbinghaus and the 'serial position effect', also known as 'recall during learning'. This states that in any period of study, the accuracy of recall varies according to the position in the sequence of the information presented. On average, people remember content from the beginning – known as the 'primacy effect' – and, to a slightly lesser extent, things from near the end, known as the 'recency effect'. Relatively little is recalled from the middle.

While the exact mechanism for these effects is not fully understood, some theories have been postulated. A proposed explanation[28] for the primacy effect is that the earlier items in a list can be mentally rehearsed to a greater degree than items presented in the middle. This additional review helps to embed the memory. The recency effect can be explained by the fact that the final items in a list are likely to still be stored in the short-term working memory. If subjects are given a task that interferes with their working memory before being asked to recall information, then the recency effect is reduced or eliminated. It is worrying to reflect that in any period of learning activity, the material covered in the middle third generally shows a very low degree of recall. Interest in the subject and use of mnemonic techniques can help to boost recall, but a simpler solution is to take regular breaks.

Take a break

When you take a break, you create a new end point and start point, therefore creating additional primacy and recency effects. This maintains recall as shown on the graph overleaf.

Do you have meetings that last three hours or longer? Meetings do not have to last ages to be effective. Virgin boss Richard Branson says, 'One of my favourite tricks is to conduct most of my meetings standing up. I find it to be a much quicker way of getting down to business, making a decision

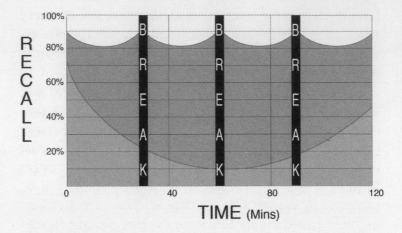

and sealing the deal.' He continues, 'It's very rare that a meeting on a single topic should need to last more than five to ten minutes.'[29] If you absolutely must have long in-depth meetings, then make sure you take a break. The same is true when studying. Never work for more than forty-five minutes in one stretch.

Breaks don't have to be long – five to ten minutes is fine – but make sure they are true breaks. If you continue talking about the subject of the meeting or check messages on your phone, it's not a break. Do something completely unrelated to give your brain space to relax. If you can juggle, this is a good exercise.

Many companies are becoming aware that an enjoyable working environment with spaces dedicated to taking breaks leads to improved productivity. Google is a good example.

Google put a lot of time and money into making the perfect work environment, mixing business with pleasure so that the staff can relax and refuel during their breaks.

Google thrives on creativity and that thought has very much gone into the reasoning behind the design of their offices, providing every employee with a space for them to be creative. There's a rule at Google that nobody is allowed to be more than 100 metres away from food, so you'll find kitchens everywhere, as well as an awesome cafeteria where every employee is fed three times a day, for free. If you think that the offices are over the top and far too big, then at least you won't have to spend all your time walking everywhere as you can just take the slide or fireman's pole around the building. If all of that's not enough for you, and you really want somewhere quiet to relax and get away from work, there's always the library or aquarium.[30]

The theory of forgetting

In addition to the 'recall during learning' research, Ebbinghaus also did experiments to determine what happens to recall after we finish a learning period. In other words, how we forget. There is some debate over the exact rate of decay for a memory and there are a number of factors to consider such as the relevance to your personal experiences, use of mnemonics, the difficulty of the material as well as physiological factors such as stress, lack of sleep, fatigue or 'wellness'. An average graph[31] is shown overleaf.

Note that the level of recall rises about ten minutes after learning, before dropping off exponentially with eighty per cent of detail lost in twenty-four hours. This seems counterintuitive. Why would your recall go up a short while after learning? The reason is that the brain is assimilating the

information. It is 'sinking in'. How can we make use of this rise and what can be done to counteract the steep fall in the graph? The answer is to review.

Reviews

It is best to review when the graph is at its maximum. This is the point where reinforcement will have the greatest effect. If you left it until a day later to review, you would have to try to claw back all the forgotten detail. Thus, our first review is after ten minutes. Immediately after a break, do a review. Having reviewed the data, the memory decays less rapidly and the optimum interval before the next review extends. You can leave your second review to a day later. Your third review should be after one week. Do the fourth after one month and the fifth after three to six months. Once you have completed five reviews the information will be transferred to long-term memory. You will be able to recall it for years, maybe for a lifetime.

You can manage the spaced reviews yourself using a diary or setting up reminders on Microsoft Outlook or another calendar application. However, there is software that can automate the scheduling process for you. The website Memrise.com offers scheduled reminders and tests aimed mostly at learning languages but which can also be customized for other content. Timelyreminders.co.uk sells software for Windows PCs which allows you to create and schedule questions and answers that can link to image or sound files on your computer.

The ideal study hour

Drawing together mental journeys, Mind Mapping, breaks and reviews led to the development of the 'ideal study hour'.[32] The hour is broken down into blocks of time of varying length, as shown overleaf:

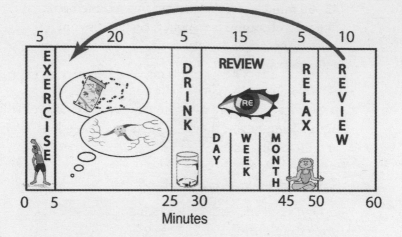

0–5 minutes – Spend the first five minutes doing some gentle exercise to get your blood and oxygen flowing. Nothing too strenuous that will tire you out before you start studying.

5–25 minutes – Spend the next twenty minutes tackling new content. This can be Mind Mapping, creating mental journeys, or using any of the other mnemonic techniques covered in this book.

25–30 minutes – At twenty-five minutes into the hour, take a five-minute break. You may choose to listen to some motivational music or get a drink of water. Hydration is important for optimal concentration.

30–45 minutes – Spend the next fifteen minutes completing your reviews (what you did one day ago, one week ago, one month and three months ago). Mind Maps can be reviewed in as little as ninety seconds so you should have time to cover quite a lot.

45–50 minutes – Take another five-minute break. Practise relaxation techniques, such as the one below. These will be very useful to help you keep calm in exams.

50–60 minutes – Spend the last ten minutes reviewing and completing the new material covered at the beginning of the hour. Identify connections and fill in any gaps.[33]

Simple visualization exercise

1. Find somewhere quiet and comfortable to sit, away from distractions.

2. Close your eyes and breathe in through your nose and out through your mouth. With each out breath give a little sigh – 'ahh' – and count slowly backwards from ten to one. With each number feel the stress drain out of you.

3. Imagine being somewhere tranquil where you can feel relaxed and safe. Perhaps on a warm tropical beach, in a forest or in the mountains. Imagine the sights, smells, sounds, tastes and physical sensations as if you were really there. Spend as long as you like there. When you're ready to return, count slowly from one to ten, the scene fading with each number. When you reach ten, open your eyes and feel refreshed and relaxed.

When explaining this to students, I often get an objection that only twenty minutes in the hour is actually spent 'studying'. The important point is that without the reviews much of that study would be fruitless. By building the reviews into the process it ensures that what is studied is retained and thus doesn't need to be relearned at a later date when it has been forgotten.

Why don't they do this in school?

According to the *Daily Mail*, 'A key study by the Office of National Statistics found that one in ten children now suffer from mental health problems including stress, anxiety and depression.' It continues, 'Young Minds, the children's mental health charity, says nearly one million children between the ages of five and fifteen now have mental health problems like depression and anxiety and the numbers look set to keep on rising.' Unsurprisingly, the article concludes, 'A recent study carried out by the NSPCC found that academic worries were the biggest cause of stress for nearly 50 per cent of children. Further research has confirmed that exam worries cause children more stress than peer pressure to be 'trendy' or to find a boyfriend or girlfriend. With an increase in the number of tests that children have to undertake and the pressure on schools to perform in league tables, is it any surprise that studying comes top of the stress list?'[34] This is a serious problem but with a simple solution.

Schools and colleges across the world give students 'study leave' in the run-up to exams. This is an absolutely nonsensical practice. It is impossible to effectively relearn two years' worth of material in a few weeks. This puts students under intolerable pressure.

Cramming works up to a point. At worst, this is a damage limitation exercise. At best, you may get a piece of paper saying you have passed the exams but with little or no recollection of the material a couple of months later.

The results of the 'Recall after learning' graph offer a very simple solution. Schools need to include review periods in the curriculum at correctly spaced intervals, i.e. at the end of each lesson, the next day, one week, one month and three months later. These can be formal sessions or in the form of homework. I worked with an adult education college who used SMS messages broadcast to students' phones with review questions at the correct intervals. Unfortunately, teachers in schools are not legally allowed to have records of children's phone numbers due to fears over child protection so the technology can only be used with adults.

When you review during study, it consolidates learning, creating long-term memories. Information is not just retained for exams but, potentially, for a lifetime. Even more importantly, as students retain what they are taught, they have a firm foundation to add related new information. Learning becomes far easier, with no stress. In the lead-up to exams, all students have to do is to sit some past papers so that they understand how they are to be examined. This may reveal a few tiny gaps in knowledge but far fewer than in the current system.

It is a great source of frustration for me that these small changes aren't being made in the education system, thus alleviating the unnecessary suffering of millions of children worldwide. Please, if you have kids or if you teach kids, tell them about the 'Recall after learning' graph.

Summary

- You tend to remember more from the beginning and end of a learning period, with most of the detail from the middle part being forgotten.

- Taking a five- to ten-minute break, at most, every forty-five minutes allows you to maintain recall.

- Make sure that you are taking a complete break by doing something unrelated to the previous activity.

- After a learning period, recall goes up briefly before dropping off exponentially; eighty per cent of detail is lost in twenty-four hours.

- This drop is counteracted by reviewing at the following intervals after study ends:

  – 10 minutes

  – 1 day

  – 1 week

  – 1 month

  – 3–6 months

- The ideal study hour combines breaks, reviews, Mind Mapping and mnemonics.

- Schools should abandon 'study leave' and instead incorporate 'spaced reviews' into the curriculum.

CONCLUSION

You may have come to the end of the book, but it is just the beginning of your memory journey. I have given you systems for a number of types of data and different situations. I hope you have proved to yourself through the exercises that you can remember more than you thought possible at the start of the book.

It is important to remember that to improve your memory you must keep using the systems. There is no magic formula that means you will be able to remember everything from now on without conscious effort. Keep on practising and implementing the techniques in your daily life. Like any new skill or habit, it will take some time before they become second nature.

As you now have a grasp of the memory principles of imagination, association, location and SEAHORSE, you can tweak the systems to your own preferred way of thinking, just as memory athletes have done with number systems. You can even create entirely new systems for applications that I haven't covered. As long as a system closely follows the underlying principles, it will work.

I have enjoyed sharing my passion for memory with you and I hope you gain as much satisfaction from developing your memory as I have mine.

Notes

1. Alloway, T. (2012). 'Can Interactive Working Memory Training Improve Learning?' *Journal of Interactive Learning Research*, 23 (3), pp. 197–207

2 Feynman, R. (1988). *What Do You Care What Other People Think?* (New York: W. W. Norton), p. 59

3 Köhler, W. (1992). *Gestalt Psychology* (New York: Liveright), first published 1929

4 Ramachandran, V. S. and Hubbard, E. M. (2001). 'Synaesthesia – A Window Into Perception, Thought and Language', *Journal of Consciousness Studies*, 8 (12), p. 334

5 Milán, E., Iborra, O., de Córdoba, M. J., Juárez-Ramos, V., Rodríguez Artacho, M. A. and Rubio, J. L. (2013). 'The Kiki-Bouba Effect: A Case of Personification and Ideaesthesia', *Journal of Consciousness Studies*, 20 (1–2), pp. 84–102

6 Milán, E., Iborra, O. and de Córdoba, M. J. (2014). *El Universo Kiki-Bouba: Ideaestesia, Empatía y Neuromárketing* (The Kiki-Bouba Universe: Ideaesthesia, Empathy and Neuromarketing), ed. Fundación Internacional Artecittà

7 Cytowic, R. E. (2002). *Synaesthesia: A Union of the Senses* (Cambridge, Mass.: MIT Press)

8 Luria, A. R. (1968). *The Mind of a Mnemonist* (Cambridge, Mass.: Harvard University Press)

9 Chambers, P. and Colliar, E. (2003). *A Mind to Do Business* (Bucknell: ECPC Publications)

10 Maguire, E. A. et al (2000). 'Navigation-related structural change in the hippocampi of taxi drivers', *PNAS*, 97 (8), pp. 4398–4403

11 Von Restorff, H. (1933). 'Über die Wirkung von Bereichsbildungen im Spurenfeld' (The Effects of Field Formation in the Trace Field), *Psychological Research*, 18 (1), pp. 299–342

12 Schmidt, S. R. (1994). 'Effects of Humor on Sentence Memory', *Journal of Experimental Psychology: Learning, Memory and Cognition*, 20 (4), pp. 953–67

13 Buzan, T. and Buzan, B. (2009). *The Mind Map Book* (Harlow: BBC Active), p. 12.

14 Lopata, A. and Roper, P. (2011) *. . . and Death Came Third!: The Definitive Guide to Networking and Speaking in Public* (Ecademy Press)

15 theguardian.com/politics/2007/oct/23/media. immigrationpolicy

16 theguardian.com/politics/2014/sep/24/ed-miliband-forgets-labour-conference-speech

17 Ebbinghaus, H., transl. Ruger, H. A. and Bussenius, C. E. (1913). *Memory: A Contribution to Experimental Psychology* (New York: Teachers College, Columbia University), first published 1885

18 O'Brien, D. (2011). *You Can Have an Amazing Memory* (London: Watkins Publishing), p. 63

19 Barr, N. and Pennycook, G. (2015). 'The Brain in your Pocket: Evidence that Smartphones are Used to Supplant Thinking', *Computers in Human Behavior*, 48, pp. 473–80

20 Buzan, T. (2010). *The Memory Book* (Harlow: BBC Active)

21 dailymail.co.uk/news/article-2795014/scientists-

identified-nine-distinct-face-shapes-five-new-groups-traditional-oval-round-heart-square.html

22 wired.com/2010/11/ears-biometric-identification/

23 Levin, D. T. (2000). 'Race as a Visual Feature', *Journal of Experimental Psychology: General*, 129 (4), pp.559–74

24 goodtoknow.co.uk/family/544585/baby-names-for-2016

25 europe.newsweek.com/if-you-are-not-afraid-ransomware-or-any-other-cyberattacks-you-are-crazy-460459?rm=eu

26 Buzan and Buzan, *The Mind Map Book*

27 Chambers and Colliar, *A Mind to Do Business*

28 Murdock, B. (1962). 'The Serial Position Effect of Free Recall', *Journal of Experimental Psychology*, 64 (5), pp. 482–88

29 virgin.com/richard-branson/why-you-should-stand-up-in-meetings

30 incomediary.com/top-20-most-awesome-company-offices

31 Buzan, T., Goddard, J. and Castañeda, J. (2012). *The Most Important Graph in the World* (Cardiff: Proactive Press)

32 Chambers and Colliar, *A Mind to Do Business*

33 Chambers, P. and Colliar, E. (2008). *The Student Survival Guide* (Bucknell: ECPC Publications)

34 dailymail.co.uk/health/article-145732/Is-child-suffering-stress.html

Useful websites

By the author

- www.rememberequations.co.uk
- www.facebook.com/Studentsurvivalguide
- www.facebook.com/amindtodobusiness
- www.learning-tech.co.uk

Memory sports

- www.world-memory-statistics.com
- www.worldmemorychampionships.com
- www.peakperformancetraining.org
  (Dominic O'Brien)

Mind-Mapping software

- www.imindmap.com

Acknowledgements

Thank you to Dominic O'Brien for suggesting that I write this book and for providing the foreword to it. I would like to acknowledge the support of the following for granting permission to use their pictures: Elaine Colliar, Chris Day, Andy Fong, David Hyner, Mikiko Chikada Kawase, Lex McKee, Svetlana Nadtoka, Julie Orton (picture by Richard Cobden), Pitima Tomgme and Toby Townrow. Thank you to Bridget Hanna for sharing her story. Language consultant: Nathalie Lecordier, former World Memory Sports Council Linguist. The term Mind Map is a registered trademark® of The Buzan Organisation Limited 1990, and is used under licence – thank you, Tony Buzan. My heartfelt thanks to the amazing memory athletes, too numerous to mention individually, who have inspired me over the twenty-five years of World Memory Championships. Finally, thank you to my editors, Frances Wilson and Martha Burley, for sustained support and drawing together all the threads of the book.

Index

Page references in *italics* indicate
photographs and illustrations.